I0030673

What The Heck is Digital Marketing for Small Business?

A Guide For Getting More Clients Through Digital Inbound Marketing Strategies

It's Just Not About Being Online; It's All About Being Found Online

By

Andy Alagappan

© 2017 by Epromotionz.net Andy Alagappan COO & VP

Marketing & Business development USA

The content of this guide is copyright of © Epromotionz 2017. All rights reserved. No part of this publication may be reproduced by anyone in any offline or online document or in any form by any means, including photo typing, scanning, or otherwise without any prior written permission granted of the copyright holder. Any kind of redistribution of the material or the reproduction of any part of it at all in any form is strictly prohibited.

andyalagappan.com

ISBN: 978-0-692-93355-8

The Income Disclaimer

When you read the document, you undertake all the potential risks that would be associated with the usage of any of the advice given below, with the complete and proper understanding that you, solely, are alone responsible for any of the matter or anything that may occur as the result of using this information as your action in any kind of business or personal reasons, and would be regardless of your explanation of any of the advice.

You also further agree that our company can never be held anyhow responsible in any matter or in any way for the success or any kind of failure of your business as the result of using the information presented or given below. Therefore, it is absolutely your own personal liability and responsibility to conduct your own due diligence regarding the safe and successful application of any of our information presented here.

This document contains various business strategies, marketing methodologies and many other effective business advise that are likely to produce different results for everyone according to the changing situations, circumstances, assets and efforts. This material provides no personal guarantee implied or expressed that it will surely assist you to make improvement to your current profits, there are various factors and variables affecting it which can affect the results. Many other elements and situations that are possibly beyond your control. With any kind of business attempt, you should consider all the money investment related risks would be based on the personal discretion and would be at your own potential expense.

The Liability Disclaimer

When you read the document, you undertake all the potential risks that would be associated with the usage of any of the advice given below, with the complete and proper understanding that you, solely, are alone responsible for any of the matter or anything that may occur as the result of using this information as your action in any kind of business or personal reasons, and would be regardless of your explanation of any of the advice.

You also further agree that our company can never be held anyhow responsible in any matter or in any way for the success or any kind of failure of your business as the result of using the information presented or given below. Therefore, it is absolutely your own personal liability and responsibility to conduct your own due diligence regarding the safe and successful application of any of our information presented here.

The Terms Of Use

This is just a non-transferable copy so you are given only "Personal Use" license to this product. You are not allowed to do any kind of market or business distribution of this product any way. You are not allowed to share it with the other individuals either.

Additionally, there would be no resale rights or any kind of private label rights provided or granted to you when you will purchase this document for your personal use. In other words, it is regarded and intended for your personal use only. Not for any commercial use at all.

About Me

Andy Alagappan, COO Epromotionz LLC. www.AndyAlagappan.com

Provides Proven inbound marketing / on line marketing search engine optimization services for small to mid-size businesses nationwide, and for both B2B & B2C clients looking to sell their services nationwide.

Your Business must get found online by your prospective clients searching for your products and services in: Search Engines and Social Media Channels.

It's not about being online; it's all about being found on line for your services!

WHY US?

We have done over 1000+ web marketing projects!

Follow me in these Social Media Channels:

https://www.facebook.com/AndyAlagappancom

https://twitter.com/seoppcguruhttps://www.linkedin.com/in/seoppcguru

https://www.youtube.com/user/epromotionz1

https://www.pinterest.com/andyalagappan/

https://instagram.com/andysmo/

https://plus.google.com/116729398054996295192/posts

Contents

Introduction

A lot of people will ask- a book on digital marketing? The digital marketing world is constantly evolving on a daily basis... and the moment it's in print, it will be around for all eternity.

I understand that even though there will be constant changes in the digital world, certain tested and proven strategies will always remain the same. Truth be told, the only difference will be their growth in adequacy as conventional marketing strategies becomes less relevant and digital marketing becomes the norm.

This book is packed with lots of proven tips.

You are assured to find solid strategies inside that will WOW you. Simply put, they are effective... once you use them. They are devised from the tried and true powerful systems that we have used in growing the brand and products of our esteemed customers over many years.

Our achieved results and clients testimonials prove our worth and credibility. You can inquire about sample works from us.

Remember: Once you use these strategies, you are guaranteed to get more customers and earn more income.

Hence, the major distinction between stable businesses and thriving businesses is dependent on usage. The major difference of one from the other is in their ability to utilize the techniques that are proven to yield positive results.

Being aware of these strategies aren't enough to guarantee you will make a sale or earn any profit. Once you use these strategies, your income is guaranteed to soar, and you will earn some bragging rights, empower more individuals, and build a thriving enterprise.

Implement this... and share your success story with us.

So, a popular question we are often asked is, "How do I do all these things?" Let's begin.

Chapter 1: How to Use Digital Marketing To Grow Your Local Business

Congrats! If you are still reading at this point, then you're already leading your competition.

Having come this far, it's only more interesting if we travel the rest of the journey together. Luckily, you are a radical thinker. You recognize the potential of digital marketing, and you realize that your business is thriving just fine; you may use the Internet to snag a couple businesses, and in the event that you do, then perhaps this guide can enable you to boost your marketing results.

It's easy to feel that the Internet won't be of much help to you. You are quite popular, you're listed in the Yellow Pages, and your business sees a good chunk of profit.

Who even scours the internet looking for a local business?

A huge number of your potential customers. That's who.

Studies of recent have proven that, a large proportion of online searches are being done increasingly by local enterprises. A current report by BIA/Kelsey in connection with ComStat, a research firm discovered that a massive 97% of customers look up the local services and purchases they make online prior to actually buying them at a local enterprise. This issue isn't only applicable to local services alone as a significant number of e-stores are being put out of business by clients who look up items on the internet but end up making their purchases from neighborhood businesses. This appears to address the issue that individuals prefer human association; they educate themselves on the web, yet they prefer that individual association when making their purchase.

This results, sadly, in most businesses having no (or minimal) online presence being excluded from the research procedure. Individuals feel the need to locally execute their online searches; however in the event that you don't feature when they're conducting this search, you'll basically go unnoticed and have these potential customers take their business to your competition, who has an online presence.

This, obviously, carries a significant amount of risk for any local enterprise that has chosen to stay off the Internet (or who runs a website that is delivering minimal conversion). Though this might seem too extreme or irrelevant, it is however a fact: a large proportion of potential customers are searching for their services and product representation online and even seem inclined toward it as opposed to more conventional media like the Television or Yellow Pages. Truth be told, a current report by TMP Directional Marketing and comScore demonstrated that, surprisingly, the volume of customers researching local enterprises on the internet surpassed those using the printed Yellow Pages, and that in recent years, the Yellow Pages has been on the decline in relevance. The truth is that individuals no longer see the relevance of the Yellow Pages, due to the ease and convenience of getting information from the Internet using Smartphones.

Initially, it's amazing, however when you stop to consider it, it starts to appear sensible. For instance, you can study your individual habit to confirm this evolving pattern; do you still use the Yellow Pages regularly to search for things you need? Do you wait to get home or to the office to browse through the Yellow Pages for a particular business, or do you pull out your Smartphone and do a quick Google search to find what you are looking for on the spot? Regardless of the possibility that you still prefer the printed Yellow Pages, watch others; your children, relatives, and companions. Do many of them still fancy the Yellow Pages? In all honesty, it's easy for you to acknowledge that the approach of individuals to searching for services has changed considerably.

What one finds astonishing is the huge number of organizations that still allocate large sums to printed adverts and the Yellow Pages. Numerous organizations can allocate as much as $12,000 or more to running ads on the Yellow Page, which is nowadays an essential mismanagement of finances; the Yellow Pages are basically no longer a great conversion tool in terms of business to make such huge investments justifiable. Reports from organizations that track their ROI from print advertising efforts, for all intents and purposes, every one of them have registered increasing losses. Consistently, more and more individuals are finding search engines such as Google, Bing and the rest useful as opposed to conventional media and research techniques. Moreover, this trend isn't just temporary. The Yellow Pages have been replaced by search engines, and they are here for the foreseeable future! A successful Internet presence isn't only a transitory methodology— but it's progressive towards a future with search engines as the fundamental tool that consumers will look to when deciding on their choices.

What that means for you

Now, how can you benefit from this search aspect of the market? Moreover, aren't online search engine rankings dominated by the big organizations? Is it possible for local enterprises to find a foothold in this savage online world?

Luckily, they can compete. Over time, Google has effected some huge changes to their search algorithm than we've come across in quite a while; most especially, they've moved searches for brick and mortar enterprises to something many refer to as "local search return" or particularly Google Places/Google + Local, a tool that was previously only available to Google Maps users.

What is local search return? Initially, once a client ran a search on Google Maps, the search would return lists of nearby businesses in the user's search vicinity. For instance, if a client searched for "Denver, Colorado", a Google interactive map with relevant markers located all over the map will appear, showing neighborhood businesses in the vicinity. Hotels and eateries were the first organizations to accept this tool and make use of it, and it worked perfectly for them; guests visiting a city need to find the bed and breakfast spots around them, and the local search return feature on the Google Maps was extremely helpful to both visitors and clients by directing clients on where to find these neighborhood enterprises and encouraging offline conversion.

In an instant, organizations other than hotels and eateries discovered that they could benefit hugely from this service, and started posting themselves on the local search return maps too. In the end, Google concluded that if individuals were searching the maps for this sort of data, then most likely a huge number of individuals were additionally using the regular text box to search too, unaware that they needed to use the Google maps specifically to find those nearby indexed businesses. Once more, study your own search habits; how regularly do you visit Google Maps in search of something? Probably, you just use the normal Google.com text box to make your inquiries.

As of then, the search results returned by the regular search box on Google were lists of links;

they weren't map-based and offered no considerable value as the map results returned by searches on Google Maps. Hence, Google began integrating the local search results into their normal search returns. Nowadays, when you look for a brick and mortar enterprise on Google, the search returns include a map too, with about seven or more areas marked on the map, which are businesses within the vicinity of your search. This is an awesome development for local enterprises, since now they stand a genuine chance at competing with other businesses: one year or so before, local enterprises basically couldn't rival huge corporations such as Wikipedia and Amazon on a national level. Presently, in any case, there's a higher possibility for your business to rank among the first three returns on a local search result, an opportunity that will definitely increase your offline conversion rate, and an opportunity that wasn't in existence just a year before.

Visit the Google search engine and run a search for your business services. Previously, you lacked the opportunity of contending in any search; but now, local organizations are afforded the opportunity to dominate the competition for local searches within their general vicinity. Yes, it is difficult; lots of other organizations are competing for these same spaces and simply launching a website and adding a few keywords won't cut it (and even, performing this procedure ineffectively can guarantee that you never appear on the first page of Google search results ever!). There is however, a procedure that if you strictly adhere to and are cautious, following the guidelines in this book will give you a great chance at hitting the 1st, 2nd or 3rd spots on your local search results!

WARNING

As we said earlier, Google has modified its search algorithm and one of those major modifications has to do with plagiarized content, which is presently more risky than before! Google has warned repeatedly, both in print and verbally, about its endeavor to compensate those genuine local enterprises with substance and quality services to offer its clients. Hence, they are coming down hard on individuals attempting to exploit the system using questionable strategies, for example, fake listings or copied content; such behavior will end up in you being delisted from Google's search index altogether, and perhaps for life. Despite the fact that this may appear to be brutal or irrational, keep in mind that the efforts of Google to streamline its internet search engine is of advantage to you; this is because you need them to eliminate the con artists and spammers in order for you, a genuine service provider who can offer clients the quality and value they seek, can rank at the top for businesses providing legitimate and quality services.

In like manner, you need to be exceptionally careful about organizations who boast that their technique is simple! It's definitely not. They'll try to convince you that it's all about keywords, and to purchase content and publish it on your website and other sites. The issue is that a lot of this content is quite often rephrased, repeated, or altogether copied from another source, and at best you'll get practically no credit from Google or at worst get delisted from the platform. It additionally results in two things, aside from not gaining any new businesses; you're also losing businesses since Google is punishing you. It's certainly not the best approach, and you'll end up a long way behind your rivals if you attempt to follow this easy strategy.

To be successful online, quality content is a major criterion, and that isn't changing any time soon. Crafting quality content doesn't need to be a stressful task, though it requires a lot of time, tolerance, and self-control: there's a procedure to adhere to in order to guarantee you create the exact kind of valuable content that will give Google no other reason but to rank you high! For many years now, individuals have been attempting to exploit the system using link farms and copied content, however Google has gotten wind of this kind of deceit and these businesses are quickly vanishing from the search engine results. Ensure you are not sucked in and defrauded by any of these promises – you are aware that if it appears to be extremely simple or inexpensive to be genuine, chances are that it likely is! Inquire as to whether their content is copied, rephrased, or shows up anyplace else online; in the event that they do, flee from them.

However, you didn't go to those other businesses; rather you purchased this guide. With it, you've gotten the strategy and guidelines that you require and will with effort, time, planning and tolerance; boost you to the first rank of the search returns for your vicinity!

FEW FACTS:

- The Internet is no more discretionary. To an ever increasing extent, individuals are making use of it to discover services and needs: You have to exploit it!

- Search is currently one of the major players in online inbound marketing. You have to ensure your page is highly ranked on the search results when clients look!

- Be extremely cautious of how you approach the search engine business! A poor online presence can do more harm than no presence whatsoever.

- If you require assistance, ensure you carefully decide on your digital marketing firm! A couple of them may indulge in dishonest practices to help you rank high in the search engines (such as copied content) however, these practices can attract serious consequence from the search engines for attempting to dubiously exploit the system!

Chapter 2: How to Get New Clients with Digital Marketing

Moving forward, now that we fully understand the significance of Google search engine; we've analyzed how recent modifications have made local search results, in addition to Google ranking as a whole, quite crucial to your marketing endeavors. We are aware that conventional print media marketing is going extinct, and in the event that you wish to remain relevant and in business you will need to climb aboard this search engine boat right now!

Naturally, the subsequent move to make is to build your rank, and in order to achieve this, a website is needed. Your website holds as much importance to this procedure as all other things, and in case you want great conversions from your search rankings it is crucial you have a fully working website that completely sees to your business needs as well as your clients' needs too.

Creating a website can be a very delicate issue, particularly in the present innovative, Flash-enabled, Web 3.0 universe where every individual believes that drop-down interfaces, interactive menus and every other kind of fancy features are crucial components of websites. this is a very popular phenomenon, where you see individuals requesting "interactive" or "Web 2.0" developers, or designers will attempt to get you committed to a Flash or Web 2.0 feature, boasting how crucial they are and the sophisticated look it adds to your website. You might be drawn to trust them.

The fact, nonetheless, remains that: for a vast majority of small enterprises and conversion rates, most of these whistles and bells do not make a difference. A bold, user friendly site will function admirably well in attracting potential clients to get in touch and boosting your conversion rate. Though this may appear strange, particularly in a world that appears to favor style more than worth, it's however real: more straightforward pages have, both as far as we can tell and as reported by various individuals, been much more successful at motivating clients to contact you or solicit your services than other, elaborate, sophisticated websites.

This might appear a bit overwhelming, particularly based on the amount of importance we've placed on the significance of getting listed correctly. That still remains a fact: being highly ranked on Google search results is still important. Actually, from the next section in this guide is dedicated to discussing that particular issue. The site, be that as it may, has a crucial part to play in this process. It's certainly not the most crucial piece of the puzzle, not by a long shot; it nonetheless should be properly done, or it can possibly destroy the whole idea of getting a high Google ranking. The main issue is this: in the event that your customer doesn't pick up the telephone and call, the entire effort and time you dedicated to getting visitors to your website will become useless. Regardless of how elaborate, how glitzy, or how sophisticated you make your site, if visitors are converting to customers, then your site is failing in its purpose, simple!

So How Does A viable Website Look?

It's a relevant question: if the elaborate, fancy sites aren't good for your business, then what is? What is the key to making visitors go that extra mile to call you?

Indeed, there are a couple of factors to consider. We should analyze them and discover how to design a site good enough to get most of your visitors to reach for the telephone and call you!

<u>Website Creation: How Should Your website Look Like in general?</u>

On the whole, there is a strategy that can be used for sites aiming to gain conversions of leads from local search results: The less elaborate your business site is, the higher the conversion it will generate for your business. Stable, fully working sites will be a much better choice for your business. Based on this, below is an overall framework of how a simple site design may appear:

- Home page

- About Us/Testimonials

- Services/drop-down menu pages

- Contact Us (with telephone and map)

- Blog

That's basically all.

You might find it a bit disappointing, and not up to the standard or size of most of the sites you've seen, and of course you're correct: those sites, nonetheless, aren't our own. A lean and mean website is what you have, designed specifically for one reason alone— to convert visitors to your site into paying customers. All other things are irrelevant; it's okay if visitors view your site; however this is useless if they don't call or you don't make any sales of product or services from their visits.

Each page ought to likewise incorporate a call-to-action. This is what will motivate the visitors to email or call you immediately. We'll discuss about the call-to-action more elaborately in the subsequent chapter, however it is necessary you be aware that for local business sites we suggest, at least, you incorporate a header or logo that shows up on each webpage; ensure your telephone number is visible in the upper right hand corner or the center right hand corner. Research report, and our experience proves, that the eyes of individuals often tend to incline towards the right corner of a webpage.

Hint: check where Google places their adverts in their own search returns.

To go the extra mile, include a form underneath your telephone number at the top for visitors to sign up for your newsletter or offer a freebie to motivate individuals to give you their email address and telephone number.

This is, obviously, only a case study; you are allowed to change up this format in any way you want. Contingent upon the services or products you offer, you might need to include a page concerning future event that you are facilitating, or current news and press release as regards your enterprise. Remember, nonetheless, that this simple design functions greatly, and on no account do you forget that: the less flashy your website, the higher your conversions!

WARNING:

It is important you don't mistake a less-flashy website for a poorly designed one. Despite everything, you need your business site to appear exceptional and we advocate a simple and friendly look. Truth be told, we firmly agree that using a less "elaborate" design usually gives better visual appeal due to little or no intricacies, and an improved visual appeal additionally increases conversion rate. It's important to incorporate the designs and colors of your logo or design that represents your brand into your website if you have hired a branding agency to create any of these for your business. Some online platforms offer color palette tools that you can enter the main colors of your organization on and they will recommend visually engaging, and integral colors for your website. You are an important expert in your locality and as such, your services are not (and ought not to) appear cheap – don't design your site to give prospective customers a bad impression. This implies that you shouldn't design the site yourself if your expertise is not adequate or hire a family member who lives in his parent's basement and fancies himself a webmaster to build your business website.

So, we should discuss each one of these pages more comprehensively!

Landing/Home Page

Although there's very little singularity as regards this page, you need to ensure that it connects your prospective clients to the rest of your website. Ensure the webpage is visually appealing, features an About you blurb, and welcomes the user to check out what the site has to offer. Most importantly, nonetheless, ensure that the blog is noticeably featured on the landing page!

This is very crucial, hence I will repeat it: Ensure that the blog is noticeably featured on the home page.

There are numerous approaches to getting this done, a few organizations place the blog on the landing page; in case you don't like that, you need to consider deeply on how to noticeably feature your blog on the landing page.

Another essential feature for your homepage is a video. Research has proven a 30% boost in conversion rates when the visitor gets to watch a video of one of the organization's employee on the landing page. Yes, a whopping 30%. Add a brief, concise (90 seconds to 120 seconds) video at some strategic part on your landing page.

In case you include any copy on your landing page, ensure it is at most, on 3 things:

1. The advantages customers stand to gain from you (not your services or 'offers') but rather the real deal they as customers will gain from patronizing your brand or business.
2. Information concerning the contents of your blog posts and links/incentives to great blog entries.
3. Call-to-action – what you can deliver in return for them to subscribe to your newsletter or call your business. Special reports, special offers, checklists and so on.

These 3 things are extremely crucial to the effectiveness of a site and as such we personally compose these parts of the homepage for our customers and put them up word-for-word.

Blog

Try not to think less of the blog on your site, it's a standout amongst the most essential (if not the most crucial) aspect of your site! It gives you two things that are fundamental to your effectiveness online.

To start with, it features the latest and most pertinent content for your prospective, new and existing customers to see. You can discuss a considerable measure of things that will be "useful" to your prospective and existing customers. Clearly, you can deliberate on fascinating happenings that are relevant to your visitors in your specific industry or range of service, in the event that your niche is on kids' dentistry then you can discuss the significance of flossing teeth and so forth. You can likewise add links to a couple of recent news articles on other sites and give some critique on how they influence your audience. A great strategy of utmost importance that most organizations fail to utilize is discussing local news. It's not a must that it be relevant to your business by any stretch of the imagination. You are belong to a community and when there is a major marathon, wedding, celebration, or infrastructure about to happen, it is good to discuss about it on your blog and include links to all pertinent details in one area. If by chance you are aware that motor traffic is hectic within a particular vicinity on Sundays, give details on alternate routes to take: if an event hosts a particular booth or show that is worth seeing, then tell your audiences about it. It's possible you will be amazed how these will turn out to be some of your most visited blog entries. It additionally gives you authenticity and reputation as an individual who resides, works, and cares about his/her neighborhood.

Another thing that makes a blog useful is that it serves as a place where web indexes can discover new and pertinent information concerning your business and the region where you offer those services. All what we have talked about before helps make this possible, and by discussing your industry/locality you will often utilize the keywords that the web crawlers will index. Besides, discussing issues pertaining to your neighborhood will enable the search engines to better understand the neighborhood, town, or urban communities that you ought to be related with in the indexed lists. Hope this is easy to see; as is sometimes the case, some marketing agencies complicate the issues regarding this information thereby making things hard to understand. They discuss keywords, latent search algorithms, keyword density, and so on. It isn't necessarily that difficult except you make it to be so! Discuss topics you are well versed in that your audience will find useful: the most obvious two are your specialty and happenings in your neighborhood and close towns. In the event that someone mentions keyword density to you, ignore them: simply put, we are of the conclusion that they're only attempting to make it seem overly intricate so they can bill you more money.

Throughout the years, we have taken in a great deal when it comes to working with Local organizations. Although we are well aware that regular blogging is essential, having our customers write twice each week aside from their day-to-day obligations was almost impossible. Hence, we eventually settled on the choice to undertake the majority of the written work for our customers. We enlisted staff content developers (great writers already writing for your readers). The outcome was awesome. Our customers get to put up great content a few times on a weekly basis... and they don't need to do the work themselves.

That is how much we value blogging and writing content!

About Us

The About Us page is, strangely, a part of the website that lots of organizations do wrongly. They're happy to just write a little information on themselves or on their partners, maybe a guide or two on the best way to contact them. This information is sufficient and does little to boost your traffic conversion. Individuals do consider your level of expertise but that isn't enough motivation for them to get in touch with you- it doesn't set you apart from your competition or convince them to patronize your business. You need to consider something many refer to as an exclusive selling position- why would customers want to patronize you and keep on patronizing you? Details about you, your organization, reason you're distinctive, and so on aren't just god enough— you need to convince them that why you're their first and best choice, and convince them on why as consumers they are better off working with you than your competition.

Imagine this: the vast majority considers one thing and just that one thing. "How Will This Benefit Me?" Your potential clients could sincerely think less about your degrees, certifications, or positions. Too bad. Their main concern is whether you can give solution to their problem, in a swift professional manner.

Therefore, as opposed to discussing you; discuss them and how they will profit from engaging your services.

That singular move, will distinguish your site well beyond the vast majority of independent ventures we come across and even some we associate with: they basically don't distinguish themselves from their competition well enough, and through this singular act you'll have a higher advantage in your chosen industry.

Drop-down Services Pages with menu containing each service is an absolute necessity. Web crawlers such as Bing or Google index the pages of your site independently.

Contact Us

The Contact Us page ought to be extremely basic. It should include your telephone number, your email, and a map to your organization. That is all. You can, if you prefer, put a somewhat unique or more convincing call-to-action on this webpage, however this page ought to be mostly devoid of clutter, basic, and be free of anything that can sidetrack the visitor from typing in their email address or picking up the telephone and making the call. A few businesses include a contact form this webpage. That is a good approach, though the most essential part is adding a clear email and telephone number that is monitored and answered by a real human representative.

Call To Action = A small lead collecting form with motivation to fill it out.

Now that you have decided on the exact design of your website, the right side should hold only one thing: your call-to-action.

So, how does one determine if a call-to-action is effective, and how do you implement it on your website to increase conversion rate?

A powerful call-to-action is one capable of making clients sign up for your newsletter or give your business a call. It's important to have a powerful call-to-action, since you're requesting for data that people have come to see as increasingly confidential in recent times. Individuals are aware of spam and scams, and as such are reluctant to release their personal contact details to any website they come across. You need to help them overcome that underlying reluctance and inspire them to trust you with their email and phone number. An approach to doing this is through giving an offer for sign up or calling your business – such as discount codes or coupons for services. Nonetheless, we've discovered that the most effective approach is to give out a great report that will be extremely useful to potential customers looking for your specialty in your general vicinity. Cases of this include "Exclusive Report: 3 basic things to know before contacting or patronizing your kind of service, "5 myths debunked about your kind of business or "6 important things you should know prior to contracting your kind of business. It's crucial to ensure these reports are relevant to your business; the more specific on your service, the higher the probability of somebody being interested in your service and signing up or calling. You could choose to focus more by going local, for instance "3 tips to remember when soliciting your kind of service in Denver, Colorado". These offers could be motivating enough to convince people to sign up for your services; they may say, "Hello, goodness, what are those three important tips? I was about to go ahead and contract your kind of service next week, but I need to know your tips before I go ahead" and after that they include their email and you now have a means to reach out to them (you can likewise automate the follow-up process).

This content is a crucial part of your website, and as such we handle the writing process of the report for our exclusive customers and post it on their site (once they review it and give go ahead). The topics of the reports above give a "buyer driven" approach; one we've discovered attracts a significantly larger number of customers than conventional non-specific marketing.

We additionally suggest that you request for their email as well as their telephone numbers too. Individuals are more willing to give out their phone numbers nowadays, than a couple of years before, when it was quite hard to have somebody readily give you their telephone number. Lots of individuals these days utilize mobile phones as their main or only telephone, and hence are ready to give it to you if you ask, once you reason is sufficiently convincing.

In the event that you adhere to every one of these instructions, any individual who gives you their telephone number or email is designated a "warm" lead. A "warm" lead is an individual who will be exceptionally open to your business and more prone to becoming paying customer, because they've demonstrated a lot of enthusiasm for your business— they've basically done the crucial step, which is contacting you. You need to follow this up, notwithstanding; warm leads, just as warm things tend to do, they cool down after some time, and in the event that you delay it'll become significantly harder to make a sale. This brings about our next discussion: follow-up systems!

It's crucial for you to set up some sort of follow-up framework already to allow you call a lead inside the first five minutes of their sign up. It's key to have a working, solid follow-up approach set up! In the event that you can reach them inside 5 minutes, for instance, then they're a very warm lead; you are aware they visited your site, you are aware they were intrigued, and you certain they're searching for your service. They are an extremely warm lead, and a great deal more than some individual who coincidentally saw your business on a local newspaper or pamphlet!

Lots of business nowadays makes use of automated follow-up systems that are set up in advance. Contingent upon your specialty there are a few businesses that even give many pre-composed email layouts that have succeeded in converting email prospects into paying customers. In the event that you need to utilize such templates, it is great, but ensure you place the call-to-action form at the right hand side of the template s it is very important to do so.

We'll discuss further on follow-up down the line, more comprehensively and on its own chapter. for now, how about we get to the main item, the basis of this guide—prior to creating your business website, how about we discuss publicizing your site and making it discoverable for web crawlers to index and direct individuals to your webpage!

FEW FACTS

- Don't deviate from your aim when creating a site: a business site is mainly for one reason only, which is to motivate individuals to connect with you!

- Flashy is not better: simple is awesome in this case! Stay away from fanciful and elaborate sites, and hire a decent developer to create a simple, cluster-free, streamlined site for lead conversion.

- Blogs are a crucial necessity of a site's effectiveness: make your blog the main item on the homepage, or clearly noticeable on the landing page with links!

- Follow-up is highly important: you ought to set up automated systems to follow-up on email prospects the minute they connect with you.

Chapter 3: How to Select the Ideal Keywords to Boost Your Business

Owning a business site is great; however it is useless to you in the event that you get no visitors. You need to have Google see your website and rank it high, and you can achieve this through the use of the right keywords. We will try to keep this as simple as possible; however it is a crucial strategy to learn.

You may wonder- What are keywords? Keywords are the phrases or terms (it is possible to use single or a string of words) that users input into the Google search box prior to clicking the search button. A string of keywords like "immigration lawyer Denver, Colorado ", is known as a long-tail keyword. Once a user inputs any such keyword strings, a result of Google's most relevant sites on their search is returned; in particular, Google gives what it supposes are the most fitting search returns for that particular keyword string entered by the client in the search box.

That, basically, is the definition of a keyword. Our inquiries, be that as it may, are a bit more difficult: What keywords would be a good idea for us to utilize? What keywords will make Google see our site as the best result for a particular keyword string?

We have numerous organizations that prefer we handle the majority of their Internet promotions. When we meet to deliberate on our plans for their Internet marketing techniques, two errors always seem to we crop up each time we begin discussing keywords:

1) Our new customer will be extremely eager to let us see that they're positioned #1 for their specific business name on search engines. They feel so happy that we find it practically difficult to let them know it is not really an achievement: since almost no one is searching for their specific business name on the web. In the event that someone is, it implies they are already aware of the organization and recognize what the organization offers. They've presumably been enlightened by one of your other advertising methods, and you don't need to spend precious moments on them.

Also, remember that Google and the rest web indexes make a quite decent showing with regards to ensuring that your business name ranks very high on these search engines for individuals who search inside 25 miles radius of your vicinity.

Always remember: you're utilizing the web to secure new clients who are attempting to tackle an issue that you and your organization can handle; to put it plainly, you have to present a feasible solution for individuals with issues. Individuals require assistance with "automobile insurance", "car accident lawyer", or "home redesigning contractor"; these keywords are what individuals are typing into the search box! No one's searching for "ABC law firm", they're searching for "automobile insurance", such issues that your organization can handle. You should aim to rank for such keywords, rather than for your company name!

2) The second major error that we notice organizations making is ranking only for phrases that only someone in that specific industry will understand. A keyword phrase example we've seen quite often is "senior's retirement law".

Relatively few individuals know a whole aspect of law business, and even if they find out about this term and begin to search for it later on but for now they're not doing great at this moment (Google gives information on what individuals are searching for and although it is occasionally difficult to decipher - it is free of cost). The perfect approach is searching for terms like "How to find the best automobile insurance", "How to collect my pension funds" "How to find the best nursing homes", or "home renovation". Individuals may not comprehend the phrase "retirement senior's law" but rather they are well aware that home renovation is what they're attempting to search for; what they really need is assistance with their parents' pension or nursing care.

The most vital aspect of keyword selection that is worth remembering is: you need to view keywords from the client's point of view. It's wrong for you to anticipate they will be searching for terms you think they will be capable of characterizing. For instance, never visit your industry affiliation definitions for keywords— except, obviously, it's to know which keywords to avoid! This is a mistake that lots of people make very often, and you need to be on the lookout for such errors. Indeed, we ourselves are also susceptible to it— we handle a lot of search and online networking advertising, and at time we tend to end up using phrases that individuals are not conversant with or not likely to search for: SEO, online social networking estimation. These phrases are what our customers won't think to search for! They would search for phrases such as "I need to make more sales", thus these are the keywords we truly consider.

These two are the major errors that most organizations we work with fall for, and they are both caused by a specific problem: Insufficient knowledge. In particular, the ideas of what phrases individuals search on. There are various tools available aside from the cost-free Google tools, though these are constantly changing.

Every one of these online tools are useful, and customers who understand how best to utilize these tools will gain a lot from what they offer; the most ideal (and quickest) route, nonetheless, to determine the ideal keywords is to simply inquire from your companions and relatives. Remember that in the first section of this guide we stated that a majority of those conducting Google searches are common people; this is valid for keyword and research techniques. Solicit assistance from your companions, relatives, and associates. Have them disclose to their acquaintances what services you offer while you listen in. They are bound to discuss and explain your services in lay man English, and these terms are what most individuals will type into the search box.

Why this is so effective is on the grounds that it reaches into the mind of customers. When you give clients a 1-minute explanation of what services you offer, and they in turn describe these to a companion, it won't be the same exact words that they use— truth be told, chances are it'll be altogether different! What you need in keyword selection isn't the way you portray your service, but how customers and prospects describe it. In the event that you do not rank on the specific keywords that individuals are typing into search box, no one will discover you and your business.

This may seem a bit confusing, but relax, you don't need to hit jackpot on your first attempt and its possible to change keywords as time goes on. In the event that you pick the wrong keywords the first time around; you can still change, alter or even remove them. Don't deliberate on keywords till you drop; begin by getting ideas from your relatives and companions, as we explained previously. This approach is a decent technique to getting keywords the first time around, and with time s you get better at it you can begin working with a few of the keyword selection tools we discussed earlier to improve your choices. You will certainly gain a lot from using these tools; however they're not essential when you are starting off. Take it slow when you are starting off, and gradually improve in intricacy as you learn each phase of the procedure.

A different approach we likewise use to get better keywords is by using the "Related Searches" tool on Google. This will let you know what phrases people are searching on when they look for your services, thereby giving you a better understanding on related phrases that you didn't consider before.

The Google Keyword Tool (GKT) is also an essential tool in your keyword selection tools. The Google Keyword Tool is essential on the grounds that despite the fact that the Related Searches tool returns suggestions to you, the GKT provides estimated figures on the number of individuals searching for a specific keyword every month. This covers the whole USA, so you will need to make an informed (and often substantial) guess that just as they work nationally, they will also work locally for you. To follow our previous illustration, how about we search for two keywords: "accident lawyer Denver, Colorado".

You can expect that in your vicinity these figures will perhaps turn out quite good. This isn't guaranteed, and no tool has the capability yet to predict the exact number of local queries for a specific keyword, though you have to accept that the national figures do, pretty much, translate quite well to your local queries.

In the event that you actually need a better estimate of the number of local searches those national numbers represent, you can carry out a rough computation: using the date of the last census for the entire US populace, and get the census of your community. Divide your community figure by the total populace figure and it'll give you an estimated figure of the total populace percentage- multiply this figure by the keywords to find out the figure you need.

For instance: Let's assume you reside in a city having a million populations. The US boasts 330 million residents, by last census, which implies that your city alone covers 1/330th of the total number of queries. "Home renovation _____" gives 300k queries for each month, so we can expect your area to hit around 1000 queries for that exact keyword each month. It's not precise, but rather a decent projection and is usually close to the real figure than you'd anticipate!

NOTE:

Try not to believe that bigger is constantly better! In some cases, it's ideal to rank for an effortlessly dominated keyword.

Another error that organizations make is wanting a catchy, memorable name or in the URL. If you aim to rank high, you will need to use a keyword-infused URL.

Here's a case study: Let's assume you offer a specialty service in Denver, Colorado, and you've chosen the keyword expression "home modeling Denver, Colorado". A wonderful URL for your business site could be "http://www.HomemodelingDenverCol.com". This will make it quite easier to rank high on Google for that keyword. We know the name is not memorable, but you can still use your fancy business name for advertising campaigns, materials and business cards that is still possible: It's quite inexpensive and easy to own different domain names, and your website manager can redirect without much of a stretch "http://www.johnsmithllc.com" to "http://www.

www.homemodelingDenverCol.com" while you still get to profit the rewards of using a keyword-rich URL and have a catchy URL on your materials and business cards.

A URL that is rich in keywords is one of the main steps to improving your search rank on Google. We'll discuss different strategies to boost you to the summit, obviously, but in the event that you begin this procedure absent a keyword-rich URL, the struggle to the top will be very difficult. Help yourself by using a URL that is rich in keywords- it's extremely useful and simplifies your task as you continue with the process!

Niching

Being conversant with keywords opens up another area of digital marketing that you need to consider: niching. Just as you concluded from that particular URL, you can't rank highly in all aspects. Except you run a small home renovation business in a small community, there will be lots of other people competing for that best spot in a wide range of keywords and as such it is advisable you choose a niche or industry-specific field in Construction to offer.

It is not necessarily saying that you can't offer other services or make an unusual sale if the opportunity presents itself, though you certainly need to carefully carry out some business research with regards to niching. Where does the greater part of your income originate from? Which of your offers brings in the most business? Which services are you most comfortable offering clients? A few things require a lot of time, while some only need you to review them and have your technicians do the majority of the job: the latter is usually more lucrative.

This is the bottom line: In order to dominate on the Internet, you need to be certain of where you are heading and concentrate on a certain aspect. Discover a specialty that you'd be content with if almost all your business originated from it. This is where you will want to begin with respect to keywords. To dominate the top search spots under accident lawyer, home modeling, physiotherapist and so on at the same time is quite difficult, if not impractical. Begin with the most essential one, the precise one you aim to start with: it doesn't have to be where you began but it should be where you are headed— the specialty that you aim to rank high for eventually. Being able to dominate that specific keyword string means almost all the business from that specific source will be yours within your community.

With regards to our prior home modeling illustration: Supposing you need to dominate the keyword "home modeling contractor." You'd create a URL that is keyword-rich from that particular expression, and after that begin to dominate the search rankings with your richly created URL, focused on that specific specialty.

When you've decided on about 3-5 keyword strings, each made up of a couple of words, you'll need to ensure that those keyword strings are included in your title tag on your business site and ensure you begin with those keywords in your title tags. You should start the tittle tag with your keyword strings, continue into the area, and conclude with the company's name. Try not to start with your company name- the company name will follow right behind. It's everywhere on your site, and individuals (and Google) will see it. Rather, begin with the main keywords, and ensure you scatter all through your website.

WARNING

Try not to be excessive about it! Google is searching for genuine individuals with genuine content, and not robots who only churn out keywords constantly. Don't do it excessively! Ensure your keyword density is about 3 to 4% in the page content, which is the ideal ratio for keyword to content. (Alright, we promised not to complicate matters with terms such as keywords density but we just touched the topic; however you now understand that particular information in the event that you wish to utilize it. Nonetheless, keep to discussing on your niche subject normally and things will fall into place.)

Another, essential aspect to consider in this methodology is regarding if you're in a region where another business exists that is dominating that bigger keyword string. In the event that another business is already dominating your favored keyword expression, you need to concentrate on smaller aspects of that particular keyword expression: in the event that you can dominate for 2 or 3 smaller subsets of the main keyword, you may eventually start getting more patronage than the organization that only focused on the bigger, more extensive phrase.

Given above, are the two different techniques you need to study from an inside point of view. All the tips we share in this guide are vital to comprehend for a specialty/business, since it makes you more educated. It empowers you to do it without anyone's help, or consider the know-how when soliciting a company to handle the task on your behalf. In the event that you employ a third party company, you need to ensure it's not merely a website admin who sets up a site quickly but rather an expert who will make the right inquiries and truly help you to thoroughly consider the feasible online system that will work for your business. Much the same as the copied content we specified in Chapter One, majority of individuals are simply attempting to make a quick sale or two rather than doing things using due process— don't get tricked, and don't negotiate on any project without fully comprehending what kind of advertising campaigns will work for your business.

When you have your keyword phrases, your chosen domain name, and your business site set up, it's an ideal opportunity to build your business. Next, we will discuss blogging for better ranking and better improved local search strategies!

FEW FACTS

- Keywords are crucial; don't disturb yourself attempting to rank for your company name. Ensure you rank with keywords that receive traffic and are phrases that normal people search for on search engines!

- Include your keywords into your site, and have a website admin redirect your fancy-looking URL to your keyword-rich URL!

- Specialize! Specialize!! Specialize!!! Don't enter the expansive market. Discover your specialty or aim for one!

- Exploit your advertising tools, particularly the ones you can access: they are, generally, illustrative of your customers and can proffer knowledge on how your customers would find you.

- Keep it simple! Search engines like Bing and Google frown on keyword stuffing; don't ever exceed keyword density of 4%. Keep your writing natural, and you'll end up with a decent keyword density that reads naturally.

Chapter 4: Local Search Marketing: Advanced Local Search Methods and Blogging

In the event that you've stayed with us this far into the book, you are running have quite a good setup. Truth be told, it's possible you are doing better than those individuals who hurriedly put up a site simply to have online presence, and you're certainly ahead of those who have stayed away from upgrading to digital marketing strategies. it's possible you have made a sale or two from leads you got from the site, and now you're thinking of setting up your Google Places and Google + Local page as quick as possible and observe as your site climbs to the summit of those local search results!

We admire your strategy, however bear with us a while— your website is still crawling! In this section, we will devise an approach to growing your local enterprise expansively on the internet by implementing a couple local search strategies!

Blogging

According to Google, better rating and relevance will be accredited to websites that users consider as current and informational. This bodes well, due to the general features of the web: new content turns old in the blink of an eye, and quite often recent content is much more helpful to those in search of information as opposed to old content. This issue is normally managed by publishing new content on static website pages, although this strategy is tedious and more inconvenience than anticipated.

Our answer? Blogging.

Beyond any doubt, blogging has turned into a popular online activity and it appears that everybody and even their dog have one, and in some cases quite a few. The truth is that blogging has turned into a solid feature on the Internet; it additionally has one great feature that benefits us in the way that it is by a long shot the simplest, most successful, and best approach to incorporating fresh and up-to-date information on your site. there is no need for you to head to the database and always change copy, you don't need to manage HTML, static pages, or little alterations, all you need to do is add fresh content to your blog every once in a while.

It's particularly useful if you reflect on the other inclinations of Google as regards high-ranking search returns: insightful, accurate content. No "magic wand" or quick solution has yet been discovered for climbing to the summit of Google search rankings; for now, painstaking and diligent work wins in the end. Blogging is completely, and emphatically 100 percent in support of this approach; it's basically a way to enable you to effortlessly make continuous, helpful posts to ensure your website remains important and loaded with a constant flow of content.

Keeping that in mind, there is a base limit to the number of blog entries you ought to make on a weekly basis. In light of Google's inclination for fresh, regular content, you ought to add fresh blog entries no fewer than once every week, and the blog entries ought to be around 350-800 words each; longer posts are okay but not compulsory, and they certainly shouldn't be less than 350 words or Google may flag such posts as worthless.

This may appear to be overwhelming to most people, and it justifiably is; the prospect of creating new content on a weekly basis doesn't bode well with lots of people in the business. Looking at this logically, in any case, once every seven days isn't that stressful; that is a total of four times each month, so by devising a timetable and keep to it you are bound to realize that blogging isn't as daunting as you feared.

In the event that you discover you can handle more writings, it's much better to post just twice per week on your blog; that's the best approach in such a circumstance as this, and you are almost sure of being ranked higher by Google when it computes its local search results. Posting two times each week, is enough; don't exceed that number! A couple of individuals start blogging with a one-track mind. They expect that because 2 is superior to 1, then 5 has to be superior to 2. However, it isn't the case as you'll have a highly reduced conversion rate if you do this; 2 blog entries on a weekly basis is superior to 1, but making 5 blog entries per week is not superior to 2 entries.

Bottom line: If you blog more times than twice weekly, you can spend that time doing lots of other beneficial things to boost your conversion rate!

Blog Subjects

It is actually a great idea to own a blog, but when your blog is lacking in informative and helpful content it certainly falls short of being called a blog! Therefore, you need to only put quality, insightful posts on your blog that will increase the level of value that Google will place on your website. The following are three of the major content facts you need to adhere to in your blog entries:

1) Discuss your services

Although this might sound quite common, it's however worthy of a mention: discuss what you have to offer, not your personality. Don't discuss your personality, your years in the industry, or how awesome your business is; all these won't help you in any way. Your blog entries need to be based on quality content that is related to what you offer visitors, or quality content that visitors will find helpful or informative. For instance, assuming you're into Insurance and a new regulation or transformation takes place in the insurance industry. An ideal blog entry will be one that discusses these transformations or related information concerning them; your title could be something like "Home insurance tips you need to know" and discuss it like a laidback, insider view on the new tips that will make it easy for readers to secure home insurance or the things to avoid in the process.

2) Plugged in: Discuss Local Events

#1 tip may appear common to most people, but this one is quite a rare gem: among all the tips and tricks, this particular one superseded them all where Internet marketing is concerned! The method is this: discuss about local events! Writing blog posts on things happening around you or associating them to your services is a fantastic approach to get Google to notice you and get higher ranking on their search results page. A nice instance is, let's assume you reside in a town with an upcoming huge event; discuss that event and the manner in which it relates to your town. Assuming you reside in a college community and on Saturdays during soccer season the town triples in population. Such events often differentiates most college town- the local are, overall, pleased / upset about the coming event, believe it's good / bad for their business? Feel the traffic doesn't justify the sum of money coming into the town due to the game? Are there any favorite restaurant or must-see destinations you can recommend to visitors and in-coming football enthusiasts? You can compose a blog entry on such an event, and it's bound to help your ranking on Google as it will perceive that you belong to that community and (most especially) the blog entry provides plenty of keywords to Google regarding your location, thereby boosting you to the summit in search results for your locality!

Furthermore, you are free to make the blog post about anything you fancy in the community and not just legal matters. Actually, avoid them- local community blog entries are worth the same weight in a manner of speaking as the legal blog entries you post, and people searching for your business will spend lots of time going through your website and blog to come across your other blog entries and learn about your services and how you offer them. This aids your organization to rank higher in the region it's located, owing to the keywords and connection listed above; if an individual searches for "Home modeling Denver, Colorado" your business will come up since your blog entries contain location-based (Denver, Colorado) as well as community-based blog entries. Lots of individuals are not even aware of this strategy, and that's expected because normally it sounds odd discussing things that are not relevant to the services you offer.

TIP:

It great when you refer to your business using your keywords! Be subtle about this, but it's very welcome to write stuffs like "As a home modeling contractor in Denver, Colorado, I'm often surprised when I step into some newly renovated homes." That's an amazing approach!

Another excellent tip is being practical- Visit a local newspaper website, check what they cover, now write a blog including links to the newspaper website in the content. It's a simple technique!

This strategy can endear you to readers and make you appear more agreeable and realistic, and this is a great plus in customer relations. When people discover your blog and goes through your posts, it'll be pleasant- they'll be getting great home modeling advice and feel connected to you too. When readers go through your posts, they won't feel like they are relating with a stranger but they'll read your blog entries on the community and wonder "Wow, this blogger has character. They appear to be knowledgeable on the topic they are discussing, AND they reside in my community and are very much invested here."

Such an individual will more readily take out their phone and call your business, plus your business just gained a warm lead because you are a pleasant blogger who is invested in the community!

3) Be Natural

This is synonymous with the last tip— be yourself! There is no need for you to always sound like a smartass on your blog. That doesn't mean you should sound dumb or careless, but then you don't have to come across as a leader preaching from the podium. Your customers (as well as Google) prefer content and blog entries that sound and come from a sound mind. Discussion, stories, and narratives are everything they enjoy indexing; discussing on your blog projects you as being more approachable and easily index-able.

This strategy isn't merely Google-oriented, either; your customers will enjoy it too, just like we stated earlier. It's a normal advertising approach to be pleasant; it's the long-standing marketing theory that individuals are highly prone to working with people they consider comparable to themselves. They read your blog entries and are like "Wow! This blogger are quite knowledgeable and we have the same preferences." They consider you a normal individual, with a genuine family, and it endears them to feel relaxed with you. A blog is an ideal avenue to do such, so decide your blog entries in that manner. There is no need for you to undergo 52 weeks of continuous specialty services content; every once in a while you can do a casual, "hello, I received a question from someone some days back and I felt I'd discuss it" post.

A great strategy, if your approach is the basic thrice a month strategy, is to divide it into two parts: once per month is dedicated to business posts, while twice a month is dedicated to local and personal posts. People enjoy meeting others, it's a matter of communication; it will significantly improve your sales once they agree you can be trusted. This approach may appear a bit too sentimental for a few, but don't push it: it is quite useful, and you can do this well through blogging! It attracts visitors and will boost your ranking on search results, which is certainly a key purpose of this guide.

The main point you should grasp from home this section is to not undervalue the capability of the local connection. We've worked with customers who have used this procedure accurately, but their business blog posts gained just a couple of hits and remarks. However, the local entries and blog posts were the most discussed topics. Discussions on the worse state of traffic during a massive event attracted lots of comments, links, and views from visitors.

Eventually, this is your goal: it's why this chapter is included and why you're diversifying into the community. This kind of activities are not just linked to your community keywords and gives major index boosts from Bing or Google, it additionally represents highly efficient general marketing: it portrays you as a genuine individual that others can trust to contact, a major benefit one can have in this our current, very cynical age!

FEW FACTS

- Blogging is highly essential for your marketing efforts to be successful: ensure you update your blog no less than once per week with 350 to 800 words blog post. In case you can, blog two times per week; this figure is the acceptable maximum and blogging beyond twice weekly does more harm than good.

- It's not a must for all your blog entries to be focused on the service niche as you can switch between making service niche-type blog entries and posts on events happening in your community.

- Be yourself; this will endear clients to you and get them to trust you more, thereby increasing your blog page views and comments on your posts from visitors to your blog while also making you more prominent and index-able to web crawlers.

Chapter 5: Be Social: Leveraging Twitter, Facebook, YouTube, LinkedIn, and so on

As I am sure, some people will be giggling now. There are a good number of you guys going through this guide and coming across this chapter's title, you are probably thinking "Facebook! No way is that useful to my business."

Keep your calm now: We understand that Twitter seems quite useless to most of you. We aware of how ridiculed it has been from almost everyone, the media and friends included; the truth is, in any case, that Twitter serves a purpose. As much as you might find this incredulous, Twitter is probably one of the better relevant tools that will work admirably in your internet marketing technique.

So, get tweeting now!

Why Social Media?

Basically: Social media is beginning to assume a serious role in Google's approach to deciding what it considers pertinent on the internet. There are lots of spammers, bots, and article spinners on the Internet, and a vast majority of the links mostly link back to useless or "spammy" contents. Social media, on the other hand, carries out its screening independently: social media users wouldn't share spammy links with one another; rather they will share genuine content. Hence, Google now understands that crawling and ascertaining relevancy from online media platforms is extremely helpful, because the online media, mostly, is made up of genuine individuals posting genuine content, which is sufficiently relevant to necessitate a "hello, look at this" from one individual to the next.

A few of us have attempted to steer clear of online media platforms due to one or two reasons; overall lack of enthusiasm, confidentiality, or any other reason why you steered clear in the first place. The stats coming from online networking and digital advertising, be that as it may, is mind-blowing: for instance, By 2010, Gen Y will exceed Baby Boomers.... about 96% of them are now active on social platforms. These are those individuals that search and by overlooking the online networking avenue you're essentially overlooking their essential means of connection.

- Three minutes is deemed the average time people spend on Google. While Facebook gets as high as thirteen minutes.

- Billions of users are on Facebook. Taking note of that, the Facebook population is larger than the entire population of the US; this is quite crucial when it comes to saturation.

What you should learn from these stats is that social media is an effective medium in the present social community, and as time goes on it keeps getting better. Social media is going nowhere as an ever increasing number of individuals continue to find a use for it and getting guidance from their loved ones about amazing stories or services that got through it.

Google has been paying attention to this and reacting as needs be, which is what you should do as well. This section will be dedicated to discussing social media platforms and your approach to using them: we will discuss the best ways to utilize these online media platforms and utilize them to enable Google take an interest in your business!

The Social Networks

In the online networking world, there are as of now three big influencers that we will concentrate on: Twitter, Facebook, and LinkedIn. We are not asking you to avoid the rest of the social networking platforms in existence; they remain relevant, and in actuality location-based social networking platforms such as Facebook Places and Foursquare are exceptionally helpful as well. You might choose to be relevant on them too, as well as on the less popular platforms too, such as Google+, Snapchat, YouTube, Instagram and so on.

For our major marketing approach, we will be dedicating most of our energy to the best three among them. This strategy will afford you a wider reach and increased ROI in regards to effort dedicated to marketing, and as such it'll be our strategy!

Facebook

Facebook is considered the world's largest online social medial platform, the monster of social media; it's widely known and used by everyone; hence you will need to exploit that. The main thing you ought to have is a fan page, thus we'll learn how to make one and integrate it into your general digital marketing procedure.

TIP:

A lot of individuals are often terrified of the privacy implications on Facebook. It's imperative to understand that your organization's fan page is different from your own page. It's not associated with your own page in any way, it's completely different from your own page, and your post on the business page won't show up on your personal page or the other way around. They are two totally different things! For individuals who are scared to join Facebook or are terrified that your own page will reveal your business page, relax: your personal data is safe from your fan page, and your security is assured.

Your Facebook Fan Page

A fan page, basically, speaks to your services. Facebook fan pages can include custom pages that contain details about you and your organization. you might need to hire an expert to create a custom iframe on your fan page's landing page; you can have your website designer or website admin do this for you. Once new visitors land on your page they will discover the information contained in the iframe, which will include an incentive and an opt-in form; these will be quite identical to the call-to-action form used on your business website "3 tips to know before remodeling your home," things like that.

The amazing thing about this business fan page is that you get to gain new sign ups to your email marketing list through an online networking platform. It's an exceptionally natural method for gaining warm leads and custom advertising. These individuals already belong on these social media platforms, browsing, and during their search they discover your business fan page and feel "Huh! I think my home needs remodeling. Research shows that the #1 rising demographic of Facebook users is 25-34 and 35-54 year-old-females.

This target market is large and continuously growing, as lots of individuals want to remodel their home for a wide range of reasons. It's unquestionably the correct blend of individuals with the cash and the intention to employ a home renovator, and your Facebook business fan page will be a wonderful place for them to connect with you in regards to their home remodeling issues.

While you're building your business fan page on Facebook, bear in mind to create your Facebook Places page also. The location-based feature it has is truly appealing, particularly on account of the wide spread of smartphones. An ever increasing number of individuals are purchasing smartphones and an ever increasing number of things are going digital; having a Facebook Places page, individuals can stop by and check out what's around them, and this is a great avenue to offer them your special offers. At any rate be available on this platform, though you can be imaginative as you go on! Consolidate stuffs such as your Facebook business Fan page and Places page, and learn how to synchronize both of them to create a powerful marketing strategy!

This is probably the best information about the social media that is worth knowing and when all is said and done; you can connect them all in various ways to create one powerful marketing machine. There are such a variety of choices when it comes to managing Facebook Fan pages and Places pages that make it imperative for you to hire an expert well versed in setting up online networking pages accurately. Notwithstanding that, you have to become internet savvy and do some broad research into building up the correct online networking channels; this is definitely not something you should throw together without thinking things through or researching on them.

When your Facebook Business Fan page and Places page are done, you are ready to proceed!

Twitter

Twitter happens to be one of the latest social media platforms in our century, and maybe one that most people hesitate to adopt. It's been quite castigated by both individuals and the media at large, yet the truth is that Twitter is highly essential. It's currently the best open social media community in existence.

Actually, this is exactly why Twitter is considered so essential. Google actually indexes each and every tweet (a post on Twitter is known as a "tweet") on Twitter. Other media platforms, such as LinkedIn and Facebook, require a username and password before one can view most of their contents; however Twitter doesn't need you to sign in to view tweets by users. This implies that all the tweets are indexed by Google, also implying that Twitter has a significant influence in Google page rankings; this because Google uses the tweets of individuals to decide the significance of websites all over the web. Webpages containing loads of links from Twitter, for instance, will get an increase in significance: you would prefer not to come across as being spammy; however you should leverage on this.

That is the premise of the majority of your Twitter connection, all things considered: exploiting Twitter's capacity to create regular content without seeming to be spammy. You can't spend the entire day simply sending out links to your blog posts; a flood of pointless/useless content (or copied content) from you would do more harm than good to your page rank.

Similar to the strategies given in "Go Local Bigtime", you will need to send out a couple of tweets regarding local happenings such as events and also topical content such as little alterations, modifications that would come across as crucial or valuable to individuals. The tweets you end out will be a summary of your blog posts contents, aside from them being cut down to around 140 characters which is the limit on Twitter per post, and blast them out to your audience not more than twice daily.

This may appear to be as challenging as blogging itself, particularly when you think about the number of tweets to make per day. Frankly,

140 characters isn't that much of a big deal, and there is no need for you to stay on your PC and post the tweets one after another since there are lots of programs and online tools that you can use to schedule your tweets, such as SocialOomph (http://www.socialoomph.com), HootSuite (http://hootsuite.com), and a couple others. You can take out the time to compose enough tweets to last you a week or two, enter them into the schedule program, and you can take a break from writing tweets till when the last of them have been sent out and then you can take out time to compose and schedule another set!

Try not to simply tweet the same exact post on your blog word-for-word! Your tweets ought to be based on your blog posts, but you need them not to be a copy-paste job directly from the blog. A good idea is for you to tweet posts containing links back to your blog pasts. Actually, this is not just allowed but preferred too! There are numerous modules for different blogging platforms that allow users to automate tweets containing links to their blog posts each time they publish something new on their blog. Exploit these tools to create backlinks to your blog entries. This process is also encouraged as it is not spammy because you post not more than twice per week, and it's an awesome way to gradually and relentlessly build back links to your business blog. There are additionally modules for Facebook too. Ensure you verify that the blog entries you make are getting posted on your Facebook and Twitter pages!

LinkedIn

In the online networking world, LinkedIn is usually dominated by the other larger and well established social media platforms Twitter and Facebook. It is rather viewed as only an expert or resume-sharing website alone; this mistake is common with lots of people because LinkedIn has very good potential if utilized correctly. First off, LinkedIn on its own is great as far as financials are concerned; now publicly traded on the open market (LNKD), this platform boasts a market cap of $8-$10 billion (approximately $70-$100 per user)— which makes it very relevant, and a quickly rising contender in the social networking circle.

Furthermore, LinkedIn boasts an additional feature for us that have nothing to do with its market value. Due to LinkedIn's reputation as a professionals and resume-swapping website, the ordinary LinkedIn user is much more inclined to become a potential customer in view of the methods/thought process we explained before concerning Facebook.

1. More than one-fifth of LinkedIn users are Middle Management level or above personnel.
2. Average Household Income is around $88,573.
3. Nearly 60% boast a University or Postgraduate degree.
4. Every one of these figures is bigger than the statistics published about Forbes, Wall Street Journal, or even BusinessWeek.

Basically, users of the LinkedIn platform are richer and are inclined to need the services and non-helpful demographics more, and unlike young people aren't swarming on LinkedIn user space uploading photos of their companions and kids. LinkedIn is made up of potential customers and service providers connecting with one another, searching for experts and simply waiting to become acquainted with your services.

Press Releases

This is not actually viewed as a social media platform, however we will add it to this chapter since it has to do with managing sent messages and can be shared by the recipients and commented on; one might say, the standard of the Internet specifically is social. Press Releases is likewise one of only a handful of aspects where Google anticipates copied content; the higher the number of copied/shared a content is, the higher value Google places on that content.

12 Amazing Press Release Ideas:

1.   You talk to participants in an industry meeting, rotary club, local chamber, and so on.

2.   You contract another person into your organization.

3.   You become part of an association (local or international).

4.   Your company promotes an employee.

5.   You begin selling a new product or service.

6.   Successful customers - make a Case Study and disseminate it to the public.

7.   Announcing an office expansion or new branch office.

8.   Accolades gotten or acknowledgment from local or international association or industry.

9.   Personnel or staff appointed to non-profit or charity boards.

10.   Launching new site (give hints)

11.   When your services or products become affiliated to a major upcoming event news item (health breakthrough, new government regulation, tax policy, latest movie release, and so on.)

12. Special report release (hint, LinkedIn hint)

There are lots of press sites available, both free and paid; the press sites that charge a fee are justified regardless of the amount since they send out to Associated Press and some well-established news wires, such as Google News and Yahoo. The farther your story is spread, the greater the chance of it being picked by a local paper that comes across the press release, which that is an incredible thing to exploit. The issue of copied content becomes a forgone issue since copied content is normal in press releases, and usually the large news wires, such as Reuters and Associated Press, even seek copied content!

GOOGLE+:

What differentiates Google+ from Twitter, Facebook, YouTube and LinkedIn?

This isn't Google's first try at going social. There are lots of online social communities; however we should concentrate on the biggest four, namely; Twitter, Facebook, YouTube and LinkedIn. Figuring out how these media platforms work better clarifies Google+

YouTube – I create a video. Users can search for it and they can watch it, comment on it, or share the video. Being a search-based network, it is recognized as the most open system among all of them. Very few individuals utilize the subscribe button as a social feature.

LinkedIn – Was once: This is my CV; please employ me — currently it is: I need employment, I cooperate with my associates and merchants to learn and grow in teams, and I find/give solutions. LinkedIn is the most closed system out of them, you need to have my email, previously worked with me, or we belong to a group together for you to connect with me.

Twitter – I can disseminate information to many individuals and have it spread like wildfire. This platform is indexed by Google, and that's a plus. Lots of those on Twitter can see and follow my tweets. You can follow me without me following you in return. Data is disseminated in short burst and communication happens both on the Twitter platform (in a brief discussion style) and off the platform (click this link to watch my video, see my blog post, and so on.)

Facebook - The present lord of social media. Facebook is all about "friendships". Two people need to equally like one another before they can share data. I can publish posts hoping that it gets featured on your News Feed. No assurance is given that my friends will see my posts. Facebook manages information with the help of Edge, an algorithm to figure out what posts they assume I will like to view. Facebook pages (formally fan pages) serve as an awesome business tool.

Google+ Why is it so unique?

Broadly speaking, Google+ concerns the process of linking all the things your PC uses both on the web and offline in just one location. We are referring to cloud, most especially. We are referring to your reports, applications, spreadsheets, recordings, all being accessible in one place and all of them being a single click away from what you can share.

This leads to the MAIN DISSIMILARITY of Google+

Now, this is awesome, I can share every data I have starting with my blog down to my financial report, though I would prefer not to share such details with the public. My mother doesn't have to be privy to everything I do and my customers would prefer not being made privy to my own life.

Google+ now offers a great tool known as CIRCLES. Circles are responsible for controlling the surge of data into and out of it. Individuals you relate with are grouped into various circles.

How do Circles function and why are they essential?

1) It's easy for you to create your own circle. Circles you create can be: Friends, Following, Best Friends, Customers, Employees, Merchants, Fellow Legal Marketers, Smart Marketing Experts, Relatives, Gaming Buddies, and so on.

2) Those individuals in your circle can belong to other circles too. A few people in my Fellow Legal Marketers are likewise my Gaming Buddies.

3) I can decide to share data with as many circles as I want. The data I share will show up on their wall or be delivered as a message. The amazing thing is that when I share information with my customer circle, only those that belong in it will see my post. Maybe I went for a seminar with my fellow Employees and want to share the materials with my Smart Marketing Experts and Employees without bothering my customers, Relatives and Gaming Buddies with the materials.

4) I can set my preferences to see feeds from as many circles as I want from my list. Rather than getting suggested feeds from an algorithm, I can pick my feeds depending on my circles. This enables me to rapidly and effectively switch from a particular feed to another one. The feature that allows you to add individuals to numerous circles means I get to view what I need from whomever I need.

The following are some other attributes to Google+ Hangouts

- Multiple Video Chat. Google+ gives users the ability to link up with about 10 individuals on live video conference. This function is awesome with very great sound. It's an awesome approach to communicate with individuals for virtual conferences. The best feature of this component is that the individual speaking gets the main screen.

- Bigger picture and video display. Once you upload pictures or a video they appear to be around 3 times bigger on the Google+ wall as opposed to Facebook wall.
- The Google platform and its features are easy to use. Google+ allows you to easily view your Gmail messages, check your Google Documents and surf the internet.
- Simple share feature. This feature is identical to that of Facebook. Google utilizes the "share this post" feature and a +1 button (same as Facebook Like button).

- 1-Click to add people. In the event that you come across someone in your partner's feed, find a name in a Google+ post, or see somebody you want to connect with, it's easy for you to add them and not have to visit their profile. This has an exceptional advantage. When you place the cursor on their name, a box pops up asking you to include them in your circle.

It's easy to set up your Google+ account. Like other online social networking platforms, a space is provided to input your personal details, site URLs, profile pictures, and basic information. As usual, share only what you won't regret sharing. Ensure your About Me area contains advantages of soliciting your services and keywords related to your business. Same as LinkedIn, a title is provided where you can add keywords related to your specialization.

The challenging aspect as regards online social media is that it is evolving very fast. We have built a place you can visit to view the latest information as regards social media and the transformations to the different systems.

Press Releases are quite essential to the general online marketing technique that we chose to help our customers this year to write, post, and syndicate press releases. Same as before, we discovered that the normal person had a lot of other things to spend their time on than composing press releases. Perhaps you have sufficient time to do them yourself but most of our customers do not. In any case, press releases need to be an aspect of your general online marketing technique.

And that concludes our discussion on social media marketing and its strategies; directory listing is what we will discuss next!

Few Facts:

- Social media is a standout amongst the most vital marketing strategies in today's world: you shouldn't omit it from your marketing plans, so you have to implement systems for managing it.

- Today, three of the largest online social media platforms include Twitter, Facebook, and LinkedIn:

you have to set up pages on these platforms and set up a system on your business blog that publishes your blog posts to the various social media communities as they come in.

- Google+, however new, is steadily on the rise: ensure you include it in your digital marketing plan!

- Press releases are a crucial aspect of your internet marketing methodology, to the extent that you ought to have your marketing agency business handle such a task for your business in order not to spend an awful lot of time writing one.

- The social media world is fast evolving, and no particular technique will remain viable for life; try to stay current so as to keep topping the charts!

Chapter 6: How to Get More Customers Using Online Directories

For those individuals who began using the Internet right from its pre-search era, you'll know what directory listing are. Directory listings are, to put it plainly, an online form of the Yellow Pages: YellowPages.com, Super Pages, Bing Places, Yahoo Local, Google Places and Google + Local, and so forth. These directories are usually referred to as "citations" by the Internet and search marketing experts. A huge number of them are scattered across the web; there are, although, only about 12 to 15 of them are really worth being listed in. Aside from the huge directories which include SuperPages.com, MerchantCircle.com, Yahoo Local and Yelp.com, ensure your business gets listed on AVVO.com too. Most of these directories take listings for free. You don't require much else besides that. Don't fall for the tempting follow-up calls and emails attempting to upsell a paid option to you. Your market is what decides whether a paid or preferred listing is ideal for your business, so try out all the features first and when you have a standard for your online strategy, you can now try out the paid upgrade of directory listings. This will enable you calculate the genuine cost/advantage of the venture. A few listing places, such as InfoUSA, are quite powerful and you need to be certain your details are accurate and optimized on the directory since different directories mine data from them; within a short time, as different listing places utilize the data there, your details will saturate everywhere on the web. Ensure your details are correct before submitting.

These citations/directories have gained more reputation of recent owing to Google's local search return strategy, ever since Google relocated its local search returns to the primary page, utilizing Google + Local and Google Places. The algorithm tasked with deciding which Google + Local/Google Places business listings should feature on Google's search return main page takes into consideration whether you are listed in other directories on the internet. In case you are listed in 5, 10, or maybe 15 directories (having reviews in the locality) this is a plus in Google's ranking framework. We'll discuss review in the following section, but just know that directory listings with reviews are exceptionally useful; if your business rivals are gaining more reviews than your business, you won't appear on Google's first page but your competitors will!

It's important for you to appear on as many directories as possible; a lot of services are available that are capable of doing this on your behalf; however it is often advisable to manually do this. It's important you monitor it closely— a few services aren't top-notch where directory listings are concerned, and they are bound to use questionable systems or persuade you to skip the procedure. It isn't so tedious or stressful, and we suggest you do this manually; simply visit the best 10 to 15 directory listings, input your information, upload photographs, and enter as much details as possible. Ensure you utilize geolocation and keywords in the description box; geolocation is only an SEO expression for your location. In case you're a lawyer and your keywords are "car accident lawyer", you can include "car accident lawyer in Denver, Colorado" in your description.

How to List Yourself

The procedure to list your business is quite simple, in fact. You simply need to visit the chosen directories and their sites, and add your business. A few of them charge a fee, however plenty of them are free though they will attempt to upsell various services to you once you get listed with them. You may wonder on whether to choose the paid or free listing, but that doesn't really matter. We know that when done right, you don't ever have to pay a dime for directory listings or any additional services the free directories will offer you; wise and practical use of geolocation and keywords will be sufficient to boost you to the summit. We've gotten numerous customers ranked very high in Google Places/Google + local without having to pay for directory listings, and it's possible you won't ever need to pay for listings or upsells too. Saying this doesn't imply that that these extra paid services won't give deliver traffic and customers to you, however don't use them right off the bat.

Be careful, though: different directories will call or mail you hoping to upsell additional products to you. Google and other marketing company's modifications have left most of these directory listing sites reconsidering their plans of action and re-strategizing; going for paid directory listing is no longer a favored strategy as it once was. Lots of these directories will attempt to convince you on many upsells and have pay for marketing, don't fall for them: remain relentless, fight the good fight, and at the end you'll understand how needless it is to pay for the extra services these listing directories present to you!

WARNING:

Be cautious! This issue is one we experience with numerous local businesses all the time. The situation is that usually in a facility, there are about 3 to 4 specialists that are actually in mutual partnership; now and then, they will individually post their own listings on directories, causing different listings for each specialist eventually and one for the facility in general. During Google indexing of the directories, it becomes confused due to the numerous listings for that particular address; it supposes it's an act to cheat the system and may overlook them all.

You need to be careful that you only make one listing for your business; run searches pertaining to your business name, address, and your co-workers, anything that can give you a clue of duplicate listings. In the event that discover numerous listings done without your knowledge, erase all of them! Begin the process all over again; it's a better approach. In the event that for reasons unknown you can't erase every one of them, then leave one and rewrite that one in the best possible way.

It was once a major act to create multiple listings on directories to help increase rankings, but Google is now cracking down with all seriousness on such tricks. Don't forget: multiple listings are not good! Excessive duplicates and Google will totally disregard all of them. Be extremely careful about this, and ensure you check for multiple listings of your business!

Also, when creating directory listings it is crucial you use keywords and geolocation in the short/long descriptions alone made available by the directories. Try not to utilize keywords where your business name should be! This is the reason for using a keyword-rich URL; assuming the URL is the business name you'd need to utilize that and not get the advantage of using keywords. Google dislikes having business names filled with geolocation and keywords; this will cause you harm eventually.

This can be of benefit to you, contingent upon your commitment to this technique; a few of our more quick-thinking customers have already modified their business name to incorporate geolocation and keywords, for instance "Senior Law of Texas Business". This brings to mind the Yellow Pages trick of using A's in business names so as to climb to the summit of directory listings, such as "AA Best accident lawyer in Denver, Colorado".

In the event that your business name has your location and keywords in it, Google will approve that; what they frown upon is clear keyword stuffing such as "Mary Jane John Silver at Law - accident lawyer – estate management criminal law - Denver Colorado". This is awful, as these keywords are supposed to be included in your description as opposed to business name.

In the event that the directories provide suggested keywords you might consider including them; it most likely appears quite identical to the Yellow Pages classifications you are conversant with. A few directories allow you to use your own desired keywords, and you should do that. Try not to overdo it, this is on the grounds that Google values around 3-4 keywords; anything more is considered tricking the system and disregarded.

The following are 12 of the best directories where you should have your business listed.

a) Google Places/Google + Local
b) Facebook business page
c) Yahoo!
d) MapQuest
e) Yelp
f) YellowBot
g) YellowBook
h) WhitePages
i) CitySearch
j) SuperPages
k) MerchantCircle

l) Local.com

There are around 40 to 50 other directory sites that we get our customers listed on. A couple of these directory listings are highly significant today than they were twelve months. Research on them and pick the best 15 to 20, add them to the 12 given above and list your business on them all.

Google Places / Google + Local

Google Places/Google + Local, while actually a listing platform, warrants an exclusive inclusion here. The listing on Google Places/Google + Local ought to be the last place you list your business; ensure you are listed on other platforms to start with, give it a month or so for you to get a couple of reviews, now you can list your business on Google Places/Google + Local. It is essential you be patient with this, and even when we work with clients that created this particular listing on Google Places/Google + Local before doing the others, we often encourage them to erase it and begin again except it's part of your best 7 listings. In the event that it doesn't appear on first page of Google, erase it, follow this guide, and afterward include it a month after.

The explanation for this is that when you set up a Google Places/Google + Local listing, it searches the entire web looking for other data of your business: blogs, directory listings, reviews, and so on. In the event that you've followed this procedure to the letter it should be easy for you to climb to the summit of the listing page when you create one; in the event that you will be happy to appear on the first page of Google results, holding off for one month before creating a Google Places/Google + Local page will greatly impact your ranking positively!

Furthermore, another capable, yet seldom mentioned marketing strategy is Pay-Per-Click ads... and Google AdWords is the best of them all. AdWords is by a long gap the single fastest approach to having your business appear on Google's first Page. You can set this up within 10 minutes or so. There is a couple of dollars charged to it daily (if you fully understand how to set it up). Or, you might end up spending a lot (when you don't). The trick is setting the ads to show up only within your locality. Our suggestion is for you to hire an expert in the AdWords field and have them set up the ads for you. you will benefit more from this eventually.

Few Facts:

- There are many directory listings in existence; be wise about it and list on just the best 10-15 that are most significant (AVVO, Yelp and so on.)

- You can hire experts to list your business on directories, though you can save more and do it best by doing it yourself. A vast majority of the directory sites charge no fee. They'll attempt to upsell you other extras and products, ignore them. They are basically useless.

- Don't place keywords in your directories together with your business name; Google frowns on this except those keywords are formally incorporated into your business name.

- You'll feel the urge to set up a Google Places/Google + Local page together the directories, however don't. Due to the fact that

Google indexes data on you and your business when you set up the page on Google Places/Google + Local, it's ideal to leave it for around four weeks or thereabout and make your listing only when you've gathered a couple of reviews.

Chapter 7: How To Use Online 5 Star Reviews to Drive Your Marketing

This aspect of the marketing system actually has some individual puzzled, particularly because its customers and clients who leave reviews. How then can search engine rankings be decided by reviews? Of course, they may be useful for customers relating with fellow customers; however is it possible for them to impact Google's huge ranking system to support you?

Things being what they are, they actually can and do impact the ranking system. Particularly along these lines; Google decides the credibility of a particular site through its reviews. In essence, if the place has previously been checked on, somebody's visited there, and the review remarks additionally give a sign of the reputation of the place and if it's worth giving a lower or higher ranking. A lot of these reviews enable users to leave star ratings of a particular place, which are considered to be highly compelling: Google indexes these figures naturally to carry out a kind of website experiment, a case of if the business is in general negative or positive.

Truth be told, Google has as of late modified the Google Places/Google + Local page UI to clearly show the "Write a review" button in order to explicitly urge users to leave reviews on Google's own platforms.

As a rule, review websites are the directory listings we discussed before; Google utilizes the data to decide if you're really the best answer for the issue that the client is attempting to solve. This is crucial as the entire concept of the ranking framework and your digital marketing procedure is to have Google view you as the most ideal answer for the issue!

Another major attribute to this methodology is that a considerable number of your business rivals are just not getting reviews by any means.

It's not a must you have a billion reviews on your directory listings and also on Google Places/Google + Local listing; you simply need a little stability and ensure you're gaining a couple of reviews each month on a few unique directories

(Google Places/Google + Local needs to be one of the three).

First, you will need to have a rough idea of the number of reviews you require in order to rank well. Conduct some keywords research on reviews; input them in Google and check the number of reviews that the best positioned returns have. In the event that they have around five reviews, then you require ten and when they boast around two hundred... you definitely have your work cut out for you! Normally, in any case, some boast just round 10 reviews (and a lot of markets we have seen don't even have up to that). Generally, to successfully defeat them at their game, you'll have to feature around twice the number of reviews that on their pages.

Remember that these are complete reviews: for instance, in the event that you require ten or more reviews, draw a plan to get it over the next four months. That is merely five reviews every month and this is absolutely feasible, and we'll discuss the best approach to gain those reviews in a moment.

Review Sites

To begin with, in any case, which of the websites would it be advisable for you to concentrate on gaining reviews? There are lots of review sites on the internet, and though many of these sites aren't strongly relevant, some of them are relevant. How do you decide which ones to go for and which ones to avoid? Normally, the major two are Yelp reviews and Google places reviews.

Luckily, there's a genuinely productive approach to doing this well. Most importantly, a large portion of the work is already done: a significant number of these review websites additionally serve as directory listings, and now your business is successfully listed on the best directories online. Now, all you have to do is carry out a Google keyword search in your area and check the bottom pages.

Try not to search extensively; you won't have to search down to the bottom of the pages. In the event that you scroll to the base, you'll notice numbers which are clickable. As far as you are concerned, you're only keen on 5 of the best, already listed directories; prepare a list of your listings and cross-check the ones that ranks first in the keyword search tool on Google. For instance, in the event that you are a car accident attorney in Denver, Colorado, then you have to Google search for your company name. Now, search the results and locate the top 3 to 5 site listings that allude to an internet directory platform such as CitySearch, Yelp, or SuperPages. The top 3 to 5 on the list are those you will need to concentrate on.

It's not a big deal if you can't locate up to 5; at first you may discover just 2 or 3, and that is acceptable. This is expected as it can in some cases require quite some time before web crawlers can index every web page on the internet. To put it simply, there are around ten thousand new sites launched daily; this is a lot of work for web crawlers to crawl through, thus there is usually a slack time as the web crawlers visit the webpages and index each one. Your aim here is to locate the highly ranked ones and concentrate your review efforts specifically on them!

TIP:

In the event that your keyword niche has a lot of reviews, it is suggested that you concentrate on no more than two. Usually, a patent lawyer for the most part doesn't go through this because their niche isn't flooded with reviews. In the event that you have a rival business that is loaded with reviews; do a Google search on their keywords and check which review website is often being returned most in the search results; concentrate your review strategies mainly on those sites. For instance, imagine your keyword is "accident lawyer" and the most number of reviews are left on CitySearch, it is advisable to focus your efforts first on CitySearch.

Getting Reviews

Since we've decided on our chosen directories, it's time to gain reviews on them. First, begin with your existing customers: it'll be less demanding to gain reviews from these set of individuals, because they already rate your business highly in their minds.

It's crucial to state that we are fully aware that reviews are, based on a particular state's laws and so on, often not permitted to request for testimonials. You have to comprehend what this means because it is very crucial: you can't request for a testimonial. We are being plain about this: you are basically requesting for somebody to visit a site and leave a review. This review place is a public community where they can write their review with or absent your help. You should have some expert make you a card, check out the below samples. You give these cards to your customers as they exit your establishment; this card will include the site to visit and guide them on how to leave their reviews. This is very important!

WARNING:

On no account are you to visit the review sites and leave reviews on behalf of your customers. It is not also allowed for them to give reviews to you and have you post them on their behalf; your IP address will be a dead giveaway to Google that these reviews are originating from the same source and they will disregard it, or penalize your ranking or even delete your listings at the very least. This is so regardless of the possibility that the reviews are genuine and sent to you by customers; a typical con artist game is to have lots of individuals composing numerous reviews, but Google can now figure that out and punish such actions seriously. On no account should your customers compose reviews from your establishment; they need to use their personal computers at the office, home, or café to compose and post the review. This is very important!

This likewise concerns the rest of the computer systems at your workplace. There is a popular setup we have come across on a regular basis; organizations will have a "review" PC installed in the workplace, where customers can sit and post a review. This is under the same penalty as the one stated earlier, and we generally caution customers to desist from such when we discover such: Google keeps tab on these reviews, and despite the fact that it's not you writing them, sadly, it's originating from a single location. Google considers this as the same as individuals who employ similar tricks and hence setting up a "review hub" wouldn't do you any good. They completely and emphatically need to compose and post them from their office or personal computers; there's no trick to overcome this and it's vital you heed this instruction!

WARNING:

Be, exceptionally watchful concerning whom you contract to handle your review process! There are lots of businesses that will reach out and claim to have the expertise to find you reviews in their hundreds. Most of the time, these businesses offer almost-spammy kind of service that simply compose every one of the reviews on their own and publish them from the same IP address; this is not just harming you but also considered illegal. You must be extremely sure about experts you hire and how; in the event that you discuss with a business and they promise to find you up to twenty reviews within seven days, be careful about them. We've even observed reviews from organizations we've had dealing with that have employed similar techniques; the reviews at the end of the week numbered 20 and came from various organizations but they were entirely the same exact review message repeated over and over again with only the poster's name changed.

Try not to hire a service for this task! In the event that you have to do so, ensure you hire a service with a proven and unblemished track record. We give our customers a review process whitepaper.

For instance, we employ a strategy where we carry out calling/mailers for the customers based on their particular needs. We remain in close correspondence with the customer and play a dynamic part because of the importance, sensitivity, and nature of reviews to their business; this is the manner by which your service, in the event that you hire one, ought to handle your order. Ensure you stay in close contact with the service the entire step of the way and gives your organization a definitive control as regards the review procedure. This is a pivotal aspect of enlisting the help of a service company; remember this process whenever you are searching for a similar kind of service.

So... since you bought this guide, in the event that you will like to have an associate from our company personally review your business site and online methodology, visit www – this website provides you with a coupon that gives you full discount of this $200 review, because you are learning and actually using the strategies in this guide. Remember, though it's free, we're occupied, and as such sometimes unavailable. It's an awesome chance to have one of our specialists review your online presence.

The most ideal approach to get these reviews, as discussed earlier, is to give out cards to clients. Don't relent, as a second way is by sending out messages or mails to customers requesting reviews (check out our example below). Bring them into the fold by telling them where you rank and where your business rivals rank in search results, and tell them to support you on the way to the top by leaving their reviews on your service.

Keep in mind that this isn't just concerning Google Places/Google + Local; we need to direct individuals to a couple of various review sites. It is right to say you do obviously need reviews posted on Google Places/Google + Local too, however there is need to widen your reach: use cards containing different review sites, for example, CitySearch, Yelp, and the rest which you choose during your directory listing phase. Don't include all the sites on all the cards, as it will appear packed, amateurish and awkward. Different cards with different review sites on them is more professional, and clients will be more relaxed visiting those sites to leave reviews on your behalf.

This is also applicable to your emails; your customers may own old accounts on the chosen review platforms and this will make it much simpler for them to post a review on how amazing your service is! This is even better owing to the fact that reviews with genuine identity are regarded highly than those left anonymously!

Once more, it's crucial to understand that these are totally, and decidedly not testimonials: they are what the customers can do all alone from the comfort of their homes. Truth be told, you're only attempting to urge on a trend that is as of now taking place: don't be amazed if, around when you begin ding this you find that you have gained a couple of reviews scattered all over the web. What you're aiming to do is simply empowering this trend: you're announcing "Hello, there are some review platforms out there and leaving reviews is positive for our business. You can leave one right now, and in case you were satisfied patronizing us, your review will boost our search ranking and help more individuals find our business!"

You'll discover, quite easily, that individuals are very eager to assist you in such a manner! They'll visit these review platforms and post reviews on your business, which is very helpful: it's a major necessity to rank high on the Google Places/Google + Local platforms, and when your business get this stream of reviews regularly you're guaranteed of a steady rise to #1 on search results!

Few Facts:

- Reviews are highly essential, and ought not to be neglected: research on review platforms and discover which ones are worth using.

- Ensure you have set up a system that will motivate clients to leave reviews about your business: this is not the same as testimonials!

- On no account should you set up a computer station for your clients to post reviews on your business (and you are not to compose or post reviews on their behalf). Google expects the customers to write and post the reviews from computers outside your workplace, thus the clients should post the reviews from elsewhere other than your own PC!

- Be cautious when hiring an agency to handle your review postings: a few agencies will guarantee large numbers of reviews only to compose duplicitous reviews and extremely harm your business Google rank!

Chapter 8: How to use Follow up Automation to Do Your Work For You

Follow-up systems are a fundamental part of any digital marketing process, and it's quite imperative that you make the process as automated as you possibly can; lots of organizations attempt to manually do this, however the cost of manually doing this isn't practical for many of them. It's crucial not to spend all your time checking and answering emails one after the other; we've worked with customers before that actually sent out their email newsletters manually. They also had to manually add new sign ups to their email list.

Using a manual system may work at first, but it's quite clear that it hardly does any better at scaling up; your business requires an automated follow-up technique that aside from giving great quality additionally scales up well, allowing you to do other things and ensuring your digital marketing procedure is working seamlessly and proficiently!

Follow-up System

To begin with, we need to discuss a follow-up system: when we discuss about follow-up, we're also referring to the generated traffic you get. We aren't referring to those that walked in the door of their own freewill. We're referring to the follow-up you need to do when an individual discovers your business; you have to set up a follow-up system regardless of whether the connection was made by email, telephone, or through the business site.

Once a potential customer visits your site and decides to sign up with their name, email address, and telephone number, they join your funnel. This funnel is a setup that collects potential leads on your behalf and you can follow-up with them from that point. The purpose behind this is they've experienced the inconvenience of providing this data to you, meaning they're a "warm lead" and clearly intrigued, and you need to reach out to them as quickly as possible! The full capacity of the funnel is to furnish you with a system that allows this kind of fast reaction to any correspondence the customer happened to start with you.

The most ideal approach to getting this done is by creating a simple autoresponder framework. This framework will give you two specific things: it will notify you when an individual gives you their contact data, and it will also send a message to them instantly. There are quite a few approaches to setting this up, and further down the road we will discuss the various strategies like direct voice messages and text messages. The most conventional and popular autoresponse, in any case, is a simple email, which is something they ought to receive instantly. An ordinary autoresponse email format could be similar to this:

That is a case of some kind of response they ought to receive right after they give you their personal information on your website. Lots of services are available that offer these sorts of autoresponder frameworks. Regardless of which service you decide to work with, be certain that whatever system they are offering can successfully collect information, arrange them in a sorted manner, and simplifies the process of automating and sending out autoresponder messages.

You additionally need to set up a process for collecting telephone numbers. In the event that somebody provides you with their telephone number, you ought to email him or her immediately, as well as email one of your office staff immediately with a note saying "Hello, this individual called and asked about this. Here's their phone number." The explanation behind this is that the web never sleeps; it doesn't shutdown, it's constantly accessible, and your site gets to receive visitors all day and all night. Your working hours, on the other hand, are just daytime hours; if you work from 9am to 4pm, for instance, there is no way you will be answering office telephones at 11pm.

The purpose behind contacting your office staff is that in the event that some individual leaves their information during the evening, they get a prompt email; when your staff resumes work the next day at 9am, they will discover the email and understand that somebody reached out to your business. They would then be able to give them a call and say "Hello, this is Alex Sanders from Smith and Sanders. I noticed you downloaded our free report and I hope you found it helpful. I'm simply reaching out to inquire as to whether there's any way we can assist you." This follow-up is very personal to a warm lead, accentuating the personal. We try to emphasize this as much as possible. Your business caters to the local populace mostly and you need to connect personally with clients to get their business. The greater the connection you make, the better; sending an automated email should be seen as the first step. Considering that they underwent the inconvenience of giving their email and phone number to you, it's only nice for you to express profound gratitude, email them back, and add a free report; possibly email them after a couple of days with a different message. You need to automate this process; you can get a couple of email templates for this purpose that can be filled and sent to your warm leads.

It's crucial to make use of this telephone/email framework and utilize it frequently. We don't run an internet business, and as such won't make any online deals; no shopping cart is included, no spur of the moment purchase button that will mysteriously attract customers with you working for it. You run a local business, and we offer local digital marketing, so you can't simply reply emails and then wait for the magic to happen. You have to understand that getting a telephone call or office visit is necessary for you to close any deal!

Another effective approach is by sending out newsletters containing one blog entry on a monthly basis. Simply choose a post on your blog, any one you like, and blast it to those on your email list. It's not difficult to blast out what's known as a "broadcast message" to your email lists to anyone still ticked as open to getting correspondence from you. Why this is important, in general, is that it is an internet marketing technique that is considered a long-term technique; your customers might be supposing they require legal services however they may not require them yet. That doesn't imply that they won't eventually require them, and these intermittent messages will remind them of your service. This is known as "top of mind awareness" in advertising; you need to be on the mind of customers with time. This is because one day they might think "Gracious! My father needs a car accident lawyer. I've been receiving messages from an agency round the block that handles such problems. Perhaps I'll call them and check whether they can solve our problems!"

Few Facts:

- It is crucial to follow-up; however it's also vital to use an automated follow-up process: you shouldn't be manually sending out follow-up mails or newsletters, or manually adding people to your lists.

- Don't simply follow-up with leads only when they sign up: you need to follow-up in the workplace too. This means a staff reaches out to the lead at the earliest opportunity, while they're yet warm, and demonstrates to the lead that you're well-disposed and prepared to work with them.

- It's vital to maintain ongoing rapport with your customers: blast a newsletter contain one of your blog entries once every month, so as to ensure your business remains fresh in their minds.

Chapter 9: ROI and How To Ensure Your Revenue Exceeds Your Expenditure

According to some ordinary marketing strategies that we've witnessed customers doing, a large part of the marketing budget is spent in the Yellow Pages together with some Radio and TV commercials; these are by far the most common strategies with most customers that we've dealt with. They hardly spend much on internet marketing, and when they do, it's an augmentation of the Yellow Pages that is hard to keep track of and usually insufficient.

Online marketing, nonetheless, holds a higher potential over conventional marketing strategies which are typically utilized by majority of organizations: it's remarkably simple to keep track of the whole online procedure. You can monitor quite well the happenings in every phase of the process: who signed up, what's in the funnel, what's happening, and so on. This is extremely hard to accomplish with ordinary marketing processes; usually, the sole technique for correspondence that conventional marketing solution gives you is a telephone number. Except you need to know how they got to find your business or making a different telephone number for every promotion (which is, incidentally, a great technique; to be explained later), you're getting insubstantial details on how your marketing plan is promoting your business!

As opposed to these conventional promoting techniques, you can gather tremendous amount of information online and from the tools at your disposal. You can monitor the number of visits, and the searched keywords that landed them on your website. In the event that they came from visiting your Google Places/Google + Local profile, you will know at once, as well as who visited, how and how. A few directory listing platforms feature tracking capabilities also; the king in this domain, in any case, is Google Analytics.

Google Analytics is certainly a necessity for any website. In the event that it's not part of your company site, request that your website admin incorporate Google Analytics with your webpage; in the event that he can't, then you need to hire a new website admin. This should convey the vital role Google Analytics plays s regards your ROI (Return on Investment). It keeps track of your visitors, clicks, information entered, the average time spent on your site by visitors, your site lead conversion rate and lots more!

SCREENSHOT: GOOGLE ANALYTICS

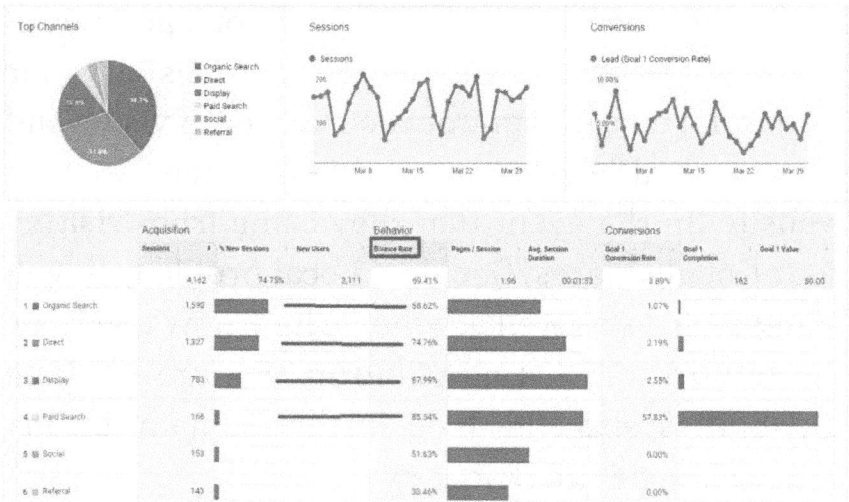

It's a very important tool for keeping track of your website lead conversion and ROI, and you need to integrate it.

So, just as before, you're a car accident lawyer, right? Not an internet marketing nerd. Although it is quite important to keep track of hits and calls (it is important you know where your finances is going), we discovered that a lot of lawyers have very little time to commit to this process on a regular schedule. That is the reason we provide a system where we monitor all activities on the website of our private customers, on their behalf... as well as most of the incoming calls via our call tracking from the online marketing to their workplace. At month ending, we send them a comprehensive report on every one of the activities.

Earlier, we said something about using unique telephone numbers for each promotion; this makes it easier to track on the web. There are some websites that give you the capability to create various working forwarding numbers that will in turn all forward to your genuine phone number; the contrasting factor is that the call logs are only available on the web and you can without any difficulty view the number of calls coming into any of the numbers used. This doesn't imply that you should dispose of your present telephone number, please retain it. These phone numbers only forward to other numbers alone; customers can still reach you using your old phone number.

Google Webmaster Tools is another useful tool, particularly since it gives you an exact number of individuals who are connecting with you from all over the web and as such tells you the extent of effectiveness of your Internet marketing procedure. This ought to be supplemented by numbers on your autoresponders and email funnel— you ought to have the capacity to view the number of individuals who are receiving/opening your messages and monitor that also. In addition to this, you also get your own internal CRM (Customer Relationship Management framework): the fee you're charging clients, your working hours, and the amount of time you spend with every customer, and so on. And as is quite obvious, this a fundamental approach to calculating your ROI.

Based on that, we believe you as of now have an internal CRM set up as it is a defining factor for this procedure and many more. Explaining the procedure and tools necessary to handle internal

CRM is exceeds the aim of this guide, and there are lots of resources accessible that will assist you and support the implementation of your personal CRM; it's an important phase in the circle, and you have to own one in order to correctly figure out your return on investment (ROI).

There are countless things you can monitor on the internet to successfully calculate your ROI, and in case need to learn anything from this chapter, this is it: it's crucial that the system you have working for you is solid, steady, and well set up to effectively measure your ROI. The vast majority of the customers we connect with trust they have a procedure set up, yet when it's thoroughly examined it falls apart. It's a decent move in the right direction that they have set up a system at least— it's ideal and a good marketing strategy. They're burning through their budget, and it's important for them to see where their cash is being spent and how it benefits their goals. For an online marketing procedure, nonetheless, you have to make extra efforts: you should be getting the data that details your entire customer's point of entry.

A sample of the monthly summary may appear like this: altogether, 169 individuals visited our business website for the month. Out of the 169 visits, 45 originated from Google Places/Google + Local, another 110 came from Google organic search results, and Facebook fan pages helped pull in 14. Out of the total visits, we followed-up on every one of them; of those we followed-up on, 35 deals were made, and every single one of them was worth an average of $1000.

This is extremely fundamental, and these figures are essentially sample figures; however it ought to offer you a way out on how to study and monitor your online marketing procedure. This enables you to truly get a precise feeling of its worth from customers that discover you on the web: Are they as valuable as those clients who discovered you through posters or word-of-mouth? We need to ensure that you're getting ROI data from those online customers, and these figures are important for you to keep track of. Regularly, we have to help customers build new frameworks and strategies to get correct reports; ensure that when deciding your digital marketing technique, you choose the measurements you want to utilize and exactly how you will keep track of them!

We must emphasize this point as much as possible: it's crucial that you fully know the figures of your online ROI always. Effective and precise tracking in this domain affords you an unequal benefit over conventional media; this will give you information to the last dime if your online expenses are yielding good ROI. Truth be told, we let the majority of our customers know that in the event that they fail to get no less than thrice their ROI as regards their online marketing process then something is certainly amiss. Normally, it not just that; thrice the ROI is our absolute minimum for customers to gain. In case you're getting anything less, it implies something's amiss and you have to backpedal and evaluate your technique again. It is possible that you omitted a step, or your chosen niche is highly saturated and you have to seek another view or another professional to enable you control the market.

Monitoring your ROI additionally provides you with another benefit: in case you decide to contract a marketing firm for your digital marketing process, you are able to know if the marketing firm you contracted is functioning admirably or not, and this will tell you if you should continue with their service or hire another service.

TIP:

In case you're working with an organization, you ought to totally expect them to furnish you with these ROI reports. They can get them, and on the off chance that they're not offering them to you or claim they're not able get them there's something truly wrong; they're either concealing something or they're essentially not on a par with you thought they were!

Fully comprehending the ins and out of your ROI, your Analytics, and utilizing only web-based telephone numbers; these things basically emphasize the strategy that you ought to consistently follow for your online marketing procedure: utilize every resource and tool you can to fully understand how your money is being spent and if your internet advertising strategy is actually generating revenue. The better you control over data flow and data tracking, the more profitable your advertising system will be and, eventually, the more important your organization in general will progress toward becoming!

Few Facts:

- Tracking ROI that has to do with print and TV promotions is rare and inadequate, at most: tracking online ROI gives an abundance of data, and empowers you to correctly monitor how your cash is being spent and the percentage return you are getting.

- It's necessary for you to have a solid, steady, and well detailed format set up to effectively monitor your website ROI. Understand how your cash is spent, know which listings bring in the most visitors, and view your lead conversion percentage, where these leads originate from, and the average price per conversion too!

- In case you employed an advertising firm, it's crucial for you to request for the ROI reports: they should provide you with them, and in the event that they can't or desire not to, then there is something amiss.

Chapter 10: Next Step: Where Do I Go Next?

Thumbs up to you if you've read this far: unlike other local businesses, you have gone an extra mile for your online digital marketing strategy. You now have a strong foundation on how to pull customers in from the internet, your outstanding website now ranks high, you are regular on Twitter and Facebook, and you have an advanced system for tracking ROI and follow-ups that will make it possible for you to identify the channels that give you the highest profit with great precision.

Nevertheless, it's not enough reason to rest on your oars: the internet is a fast paced target. Internet marketing will definitely expand; keeping up with it will be your task. This chapter reveals what to expect along the line, unexplored aspects of online marketing which will soon be goldmines. Local businesses need to consider these things, new trends and technologies that should be incorporated into your marketing technique to enable you take charge of the game!

Mobile

This topic has been our focus to the end; however, this is the closest of all the impending challenges for internet marketing. With speed and general usage, mobile device is becoming the major interaction mode with the web. According to an estimate by Morgan-Stanley, with the rate of increase in mobiles, by mid-2014, the number of connected mobiles to the internet will exceed that of laptops and PCs. That's true, by 2017, there will be more phones connected to the internet than computers.

Frankly, mobile phone is a huge force prompting many of the search engines springing up. Google is putting in place infrastructure in local places because it's of the view that information is going mobile. Traditional search differs from mobile search. Most times it is used promptly. Mobile searchers usually have the mentality of I need things immediately, unlike regular researchers who are ready to sift through articles and answers from various webpages. Only few people will do this on a mobile device, in most cases, they are in search of a business close by they can drive or walk to with ease.

For an immigration lawyer, this is a breakthrough, despite the fact that many lawyers have stared at us cynically when we mention this. Most times, people think of their problems while driving round, talking to others or at lunch. Then they say to themselves, "I will search for an answer with my phone right away." This is also the case while watching TV or eating dinner, it is likely that their phones are handy or on the table near them. Instead of postponing the answer to their problem, they just make use of their mobile phone to find answers.

This is not something strange, think about how you use your mobile phone and also how you have seen others use theirs. Most mobile phones give a fast confidence, and users capitalize on it to get answers quickly. You will feel left out if your website isn't mobile friendly or your Google + Local/Google Places page is non-existent (Google Places/Google + Local is exceptionally mobile-friendly).

The mobile world also streamlines the ranking requirements to some extent. You have to rank among the top 7 to 10, on the normal desktop internet, 8 is the lowest minimum, but ranking among the top 3 or 4 is great. If you aren't top 2 to 3, then you aren't been seen, only few mobile phone users scroll down, most times they just click on the first or second result they find. This is very vital to you because mobile phones provide and unequivocal ease in usage, for instance, many phones like the Android and iPhone offer in-built web calling. With a tap on your phone number the mobile phone dials the number immediately, no need to pick up another phone. With the popularity of mobile devices, it is therefore essential that our website is mobile-friendly and ranks in A or B listing on Google's result returns.

Social

It's glaring that we have covered a good portion of social media previously, at the moment you can perfectly manage the social network scene. However, we are yet to cover the future of social networks – prospective change in social networks and its impact on your internet marketing technique.

This is the first and most vital part of the future of social media: definitely, social media would no longer end as a place where individuals connect. In the coming times, there will be a transformation of social media networks to something that is more search engine oriented; Facebook will be used for searches and not just interactions. This is why you need to establish your presence on time. There is still time, and you aren't lagging behind yet, register your online presence on sites like Twitter, LinkedIn, Facebook, YouTube, Digg, StumbleUpon, and similar social media sites. You don't necessarily need to use all of them daily or frequently; however, you will need to be constant with the big ones. The most important thing to you is your presence, simply ensure that your listings are accurate on these sites- you will be happy about it later!

With the passing of time social media networks are becoming location-oriented, hence, the trend is expected to remain so: this will finally result in a kind of social media combination: users using their

Facebook mobile app and Google searching at the same time. This pattern of usage exists at the moment and this kind of behavior is presently on the rise and common at the moment. While using the Facebook app users can visit places listing and check what is near them. This is usually very helpful to bars and restaurants, and they are making good use of it, it is also cool for businesses too: by writing office locations users can simply recall the addresses. Having this local presence is a necessity because failure to do so will make it impossible to find you, and somebody else will seize the opportunity!

This social/ search combo we are witnessing its gradual rise will form a vital aspect of internet marketing in future: a combo of Google ranking and social interaction. Many people will go online on Facebook and find out what their friends think instead of waiting for Google to find out who is first. Your Facebook presence, reviews, and level of interaction are going to be important at this level of play: many people will search there just like the do on Google. However, some internet result will still come through; a good area of the result will result from the customer's social network.

This is essential because individuals will most likely take the views of their family and friends very serious. From a marketing aspect, it's a very popular and trusted fact that individuals take the opinions of their family and friends serious than that gotten from other marketing source. Due to this, the social combo will be more influential; you should monitor it and allow it progress.

Direct Mailing To Online Source

Are you wondering why we are including direct mailing in the "What's Next" category; in Internet marketing terms, direct mailing is as old as stone. It is here because there is definite potential for it as the year continues: like outdated fashion suddenly coming back again and becoming famous again, direct making will definitely reign again. Scarcity of this is partly because of this. Constantly receiving mail if done well isn't a bad marketing option. It isn't something you should heavily rely on, however, it's something to have in your backup and use when necessary.

If you have an ongoing direct mail campaign and want to continue it, it is essential for you to find a way to incorporate your website, Facebook, Google Places / Google + Local, or a call to action in your direct mailers; you need to shift the aim to getting clients online. Using a mobile device for direct mailing is a very attractive option; the ability to take a picture and move straight to a site check reviews or see information or the ability to text a certain number to get a special report are promising options.

Texting

Just like was explained with direct mailing, you can make people text a number and receive information; once they text the number, they will be entering your marketing funnel. All this will happen automatically; you can set up an autoresponder to send texts just the same way it sends emails. With the input of their mobile phone number they will receive a message similar to "Your email and name has been received. We appreciate you getting I touch with us! See your email for a free special report. You will be contacted shortly by one of our personnel!"

Another area of texting that is worthy of mention is: some of those involved in businesses like bars and restaurants have automatic texts that sends out newest deals or coupons, with marketing ploys like Five for Four Fridays, Tuesday happy hours etc. It's very rampant with such businesses; however, we have begun the implementation of such ideas with some of our clients like dentists, frankly speaking, we are uncertain whether people see it as spam or not. This might be favorable to your niche. Ensure you visit our site listed in the resource area for information review service and be updated with our research in this field!

Don't be scared of sending out texts once or twice monthly. Ensure the tests are relevant and well detailed and should be sent at maximum twice monthly else, it could be seen as spam. Unlike mails texts are usually read 90% of the time while text is read barely 17 to 20% of the time (this numbers are fairly inflated). A text sent at the right time at strategic times can help boost your business and make some clients contact you!

Direct Voicemail

Direct voicemail is the act of sending a voicemail directly into a mobile phone without any need for the phone to ring, with voicemail systems in phones, this is very easy to do, and it works perfectly. These systems are pretty effective; it's possible to put in place outbound voicemails that talk of new ventures and changes about you and your business. The timing could last for thirty to ninety seconds, and can be sent to their mobile phones directly instead of calling. There won't be ringing but the voicemail notifier will pop up, this makes means the client will be aware of the message and can listen to it at their convenience. It gives no form of disturbance hence causing a higher listen rate.

It's one of the key reasons why we initially advised you to get the phone numbers from your clients; it can be used for texting as well as voicemail too. Direct voicemails are usually personal and efficient, and are best used for activities your business do and events. For instance seminars- if you are organizing seminar in an area relating to your industry, sending a voicemail is an effective and personal means of telling your clients about the seminar coming up. It's simple, non-interfering and works effectively!

Summing Up

There is a reason why we gave this chapter its name, the internet marketing space is or will be affected by many of these technologies. Frankly, some of the strategies and ideas earlier discussed are already surfacing. We have started testing all these using our clients who are performing well or are competing in a tight market; this proves that these ideas aren't just fluff or theory. They are feasible strategies that are now surfacing in the market, and it's advisable to be conversant with them.

Speak with the agency you work with and contact us to know how their ideas fare on these future strategies. There is nothing rigid about them, and one or two ingenious ideas can make you outstanding in areas like this. Finding the right agency is likewise essential; find an agency that specializes in techniques like these, they aren't things known by the regular webmaster there is a high chance that they will be entirely new to an average webmaster. Ensure that the agency you contact is one with a full knowledge of internet marketing, its workings with other forms of marketing, and understanding of future strategies in years to come.

For additional assistance, kindly visit one of our local area marketing site, www.LocalSEOtx.com

Few Facts:

– In few years to come, mobile and social media will be the new marketing driving force: both are leading marketing to become more location-oriented, due to the live nature that blends social and mobile. Be updated on them and don't let any opportunity pass you by, get the most out of on these markets!

– People value opinion gotten from friends more: ensure that your social media presence is strong, and harness your social media presence by achieving a perfectly-established business that fall among the top ranks in the ever certain social/search aspect.

– Direct mailing is still a force to reckon with globally, however it should be leading clients to your site to enable you get the warm lead- it's also essential to get them to make use of an easily analyzed and tracked channel.

– Never rest on your oars: be forward thinking and innovative in technologies, ensure you work with agencies that are versed in the online field, professionals in the online marketing world, and can help you maintain your top spot.

Chapter 11: How To Get Help When Starting Off

How To Find Professionals Who Can Help You

Lastly a workforce is what you need. Sincerely speaking, you didn't attend school, pass your exams, and build a career so you could spend all the day designing websites, submitting listings to directories, and uploading infographics and new videos.

At this point we wish there is a better way to say this, but finding competent people for this job is difficult. A good number of web designers aren't rich, they have no understanding about digital and online marketing, and many have only local clients, yes, they live off their parent. This kind of person can't be trusted with your marketing to prevent wasting your time and financial resource.

Most times, people ask us where they can find web experts. Our answer is usually this- we find a person who is good (only few), and we employ them to works as part of our team.

Outsourcing to remote location business is very practical option if they have a solid track record. Also assigning this work to one of your assistants or clerks will defeat your leads generation objectives and put you both at loggerheads.

So How Can I Do All These?

First, at this point you will concur, local web marketing is very likely to be influenced by time, pressing issue on your business calendar at the moment. For now, it's still vague, but in 6 to 18 months' time when you look back, you will likely wish you can rewind to this moment.

There is enough room for local internet marketing presently, however, this opening won't be for long and we wouldn't want you to fail in securing the financial future of your practice simply because of some ambiguities.

Alternatively, finding experts who can assist you in managing your online presence is difficult. Many web designers are not digital marketing experts and many pretend to be jack of all trades. Even if they can help you set up a nice site, it's no pointer to the fact that they can help you rank among sites on page 1 of Google/Bing many times. Also, you will be wasting money and time if you outsource this kind of work to web designers, PR Agencies, Branding agencies and the like who do not have in-house skilled digital marketing experts (it's a mistake many small- and medium-sized businesses have made and won't like to see you do).

We would be pleased to offer our marketing agency service, however at this time, we have a many consistently-paying small and medium sized clients, and we are committed to them.

For the sake of full disclosure, we offer a way out, hundred percent custom tailored (not a one size fits all) services for you, meaning you send us the contact information of your business and we handle the rest. We start with a free online audit analysis. Basically, we do it all for you. Also, we can help you achieve results faster than any other provider. We charge an affordable sum for our services; however you will obviously see somebody else offering it for a lesser fee. Nevertheless, we take our clients future very serious and when your client base gets an increase of 3, 5, or 8 clients monthly at $5,000.00 or more, it's a win, win for we and you.

Nonetheless, we wouldn't be making this available for all and sundry, just a few clients in a particular geographical location. It is possible that your location has been spoken for and while it doesn't mean that we won't take you, it's likely that we are already committed and simply have to ignore.

With all these said; if you are of the view that your business is worth our selection and you would like to know more about the availability of my team to assist you and do all this for you, kindly contact us via our mini form in our web site with:

Full Name:

Phone:

Email:

Web Site:

One competitor web site:

The first thing we start with if we strike a deal and want to work with you is; a FREE online Web Strategy Analysis and your online visibility audit. We have no obligation neither do you. It only starts the discussion on how we can be able to assist you. Although we are aware that some individual take this experience-backed, top-quality web strategy then go and pay a cheap local marketing agency we don't fret because, we know people who understand the essence and importance of growing their business through the maximization of their online marketing investments will simply ask us to do it for them. We only need few clients we can build a long-term relationship with and if your business fits this description then kindly contact us either by writing or calls.

With these, we say goodbye if you read up to this point (end of the book), however, know you definitely have not gotten to the end of how we can be of help to you. If you have adhered to the whole processes and techniques mentioned in this book and really meditate and abide by them, then you are set to delve into online marketing field and come out outstanding. You know what's involved and now above your contemporaries and competitors. Don't rest on your oars, be innovative, and you will definitely make it big in the online marketing field for many years!

APPENDIX A: GLOSSARY

ANALYTICS: Analytics are technical measures you can take to see what happens with visitors on your website: how long they stay, what they click, how many of them return to the website, and statistics of that nature. One of the best analytic software packages out there currently is Google Analytics, which is also free.

Algorithmic listing. Any search engine listing that is on the "free" or unpaid section of a search results page. These listings are obtained using SEO techniques without the use of paid advertising. Also called organic, natural or editorial listing.

Backlinks, backward links. Links from other sites that point to your site. Also known as inbound or incoming links.

Conversion rate. The percentage of visitors to a website that end up performing a specific action that leads to a sale. Such actions can include the purchase of a product, the submission of a form, or an email requesting more information.

Crawl. The operation of reading or analyzing pages of a website by an automated program called a spider or robot. Spiders crawl your web site by following links on each page of your site. After crawling, the spider will return the results back to the search engine for later inclusion into its database for indexing.

Deep crawl. Deep crawls are performed once a month by the main Google spider Googlebot; all pages of a site are visited during a deep crawl. Also known as the main crawl.

Directory. As opposed to search engines, search directories use humans to review and place websites in alphabetical order under defined categories and sub-categories. The best-known directories are Yahoo! and the Open Directory Project (OPD).

FreshBot. A version of the Google spider that visits high-ranking sites, or sites that change content frequently. Freshbot may visit sites daily, while Googlebot visits sites once a month.

Fresh crawl. Fresh crawls are performed as often as daily by the Google spider Freshbot. Freshbot only crawls portions of your site and looks for new pages and updated content on existing pages only.

Google AdWordsTM. Google's Pay-Per-Click (PPC) advertising program, whereby your site is listed in the right-hand side of Google search result pages in a small box. For every visitor that clicks on your AdWords link, you pay Google a fee, up a maximum daily limit. This type of advertising involves an auction where you bid, along with your competitors, for the cost per click for a specific keyword.

Google DirectoryTM. The Google Directory lists those websites that are in the Open Project Directory (OPD), and then ranks them according to PageRank alone.

Google ToolbarTM. A downloadable program that attaches to your browser, allowing you to see an approximation for the PageRank (PR) value of a page, along with the external sites that link to that page.

Inbound, incoming links. Links that reside on another website that point to your website. Also known as backlinks or backward links. The opposite of inbound links are outbound links.

Index. Term used to denote the database that stores information about every web page for every website that a search engine has crawled (visited). If your website is included in the Google database (index), it is said to be indexed.

Index page. Another name for a home page. Many home pages are named http://seohoustonweb.com so that Web servers will display this page by default.

Keyword phrase. General term used to define a specific word phrase that best describes the main topic of a web page. Synonymous with a search phrase that a visitor enters into a search engine to find specific information.

Keyword. General term used to define the main topic of a page. Synonymous with search term. A group of keywords used together in a phrase is called a keyword phrase. Google looks for keywords on a page that match searched-for terms.

Keyword density. The number of times a keyword is used on a web page divided by the total number of words on the page. Expressed as a percentage.

Landing page. Generally speaking, the web page that a person reaches when clicking on a search engine listing or ad. This is commonly the home page of the site but it can be any. For paid advertising, it is common to have multiple ads, each one linking to a specific web page on the site that is targeted specifically for that ad.

Link quality. A general term referring to link reputation and link strength. Links with high quality are those where the PageRank of the linking page is high, and where your keywords are used in the link text and in the page title that the link is.

Main crawl. Main crawls are performed once a month by the main Google spider Googlebot; all pages of a site are crawled during a main crawl. Also known as the deep crawl.

META tags. HTML tags located in the section of a web page that specify information that is viewable only to a search engine. The two most commonly-used META tags are the "keywords" META tag and the "description" META tag.

Natural Organic listing. Any search engine listing that is on the "free" or unpaid section of a search results page. These listings are obtained using SEO techniques without the use of paid advertising. Also called organic, algorithmic or editorial listing.

Off-page factors. Those aspects or elements of a website which are not located on your website (such as incoming links). Off-page factors are largely out of your control.

On-page factors. Those aspects or elements of a website which are located on your website (such as keywords). You are largely in control of on-page factors

PageRankTM. Google's patented system for measuring page importance. PageRank analyzes the quantity and quality of links that point to a web page. The more high-quality links that point to your web page from other sites, the higher your PageRank is.

Pay-Per-Click (PPC). A paid advertising mechanism whereby you bid to have your site listed in a specific position on a search engine. You bid, along with your competitors, for the cost per click of a specific keyword. Every time a visitor clicks on your listing (ad), you pay the PPC company the bid price. Google AdWords is the name of the PPC program that Google offers.

Rank, ranking. a website's actual placement or position on a search engine results page for a certain search term or phrase.

Robot. The software program which a search engine runs to read and analyze your site. See also spider. Google's robots are called Googlebot and Freshbot.

Search Engine Marketing (SEM). A general term that encompasses both paid and free forms of advertising a website using search engines. Often used interchangeably with Search Engine Optimization (SEO). SEO is actually one type of SEM. The other major type of SEM is Pay-Per-Click advertising (PPC).

Search Engine Optimization (SEO). A general term used to describe specific techniques that can be used on websites in order to rank favorably with search engine. A good example of SEO is the proper use of keywords in specific locations on a web page.

Search Engine Positioning (SEP). A general term used interchangeably with SEO. However, since search engine optimizers do not actually "position" pages within the search engines, this can be misleading. SEP more closely describes Pay-Per-Click (PPC) advertising, since that is the only way a site can be exactly positioned in a search engine.

SERP. Search Engine Results Page. The page or pages that a search engine displays after a search query for a certain search term or phrase.

Server log. The data file that a Web server produces (usually daily) that lists website traffic activity by domain. Web statistics programs use the server log file to produce graphic reports.

Spider. The software program, also known as a robot, which a search engine runs to read through and analyze your site. Google's spiders are called Googlebot and Freshbot.

Tracking URL. Typically used in paid ads, such as Google AdWords, where unique code is added to the end of a link in order to track visitors who click on that ad. Tracking URLs allow you to measure the popularity of an ad.

Vote, voting. When one website links to another website, it "casts a vote" for the other website. The strength or weight of this "vote" depends on the PageRank of the page and the number of other links on the page.

Yahoo! A popular search directory (as opposed to a search engine). All Web sites listed on Yahoo are first reviewed by a human editor.

LOCAL SEARCH RETURN: A feature within Google's search engine that returns location-specific results for a user who types in keywords that relate to local businesses. For example, a local search return would appear for a user in Houston, Texas who typed in "immigration law." A map and local businesses that are relevant to the search result would appear in the ensuing search page.

UNIQUE SELLING POSITION (USP): Unique Selling Position separates you from your competition in a specific market place. The term is often used to refer to any aspect of an object that differentiates it from similar objects.

URL: An acronym for "Uniform Resource Locator". It is the name that the user types into the browser bar in order to access a specific website; for example, "www.Google.com" or "www.bing.com" would be examples of URLs.

Our books are found at the following booksellers.

If you would you like to offer this book at your next event or association meeting, we offer quantity discounts. For more information please contact: getseen@gmail.com

BONUS!

Discover Exactly How a Few Adjustments will you Begin to Dominate Local Search Results...It All Starts with Your Free online visibility Review.

http://www.WebsiteLeadsAgency.com

If you want our Your Free on line visibility Review visit this link. There is no obligation on either your or our part. This just begins the discussion as to how we may be able to help you. This URL and the sign up form in it gives you a coupon that makes this 0 review free for you, since you are reading and implementing the things in this book. Note, while it's free, we're busy, the availability may be limited. It's a great opportunity to get your online presence reviewed by one of our experts.

And while we know that some people take this experience-backed, high-quality web strategy then go and hire a cheap local marketing agency, we also know that the best customers, those who understand the value of growing their business by maximizing their online marketing investment will ask us to just "do it for me." We are always on the lookout for high quality clients to build a long-term relationship with. And if that sounds like your business, then please feel free to write or call.

For more information, call 832-677-4620 or email us: visit: www.AndyAlagappan.com

Thank you!

www.ingramcontent.com/pod-product-compliance
Lightning Source LLC
Chambersburg PA
CBHW050110210326
41519CB00015BA/3905